SPIRITUAL

JIHAD

T. KOBELT

Word Alive Press
119 De Baets Street, Winnipeg, MB R2J 3R9
www.wordalivepress.ca

Cataloguing in Publication may be obtained through Library and Archives Canada

CONTENTS

INTRODUCTION

Jihad is the struggle for supremacy on three fronts. The first battlefront is for the supremacy of our minds. We will explore the personal theological tools necessary to fight that good fight. The greater Jihad is the battle for our being. The second battlefront emerges as a result of victory or defeat on the first front. It is the public battle we face day by day as we go out to "do battle" on the world stage. It can be seen as we verbally joust with others or as we choose to keep peace. The third battlefront knits us together as a fellowship where we, as a group, unite under a common banner to witness and wage warfare against a common enemy. It is the third battle, the lesser Jihad, that makes for newspaper headlines; yet the loss and the victories recorded on the headlines were predetermined though the battle of the greater Jihad.

"God does not play dice with the universe" is a quote attributed to Albert Einstein. While the theoretical physicist made a statement of a fundamental assumption of his work and life philosophy, he also made a statement about an attribute of God. We do not have to be intellectual giants like Einstein to make a comment about God, since in essence we are all theologians. While our theology may not be tested to the degree or rigor of a professor of Old Testament or the local rabbi, each of us has developed a personal philosophy and theology. Our philosophy of life and our theology, whether stated explicitly or implied, become the bedrock and foundation for our actions in life.

As we go through our life we collect experiences. History is that recorded collection of experiences. Beyond the recorded history is the personal history of each individual on this planet. Each person has a story. Each story is full of decisions and consequences. The choices made in each story reflect our desires for relationships and objects. Hollywood is full of stories made larger than life where the guy gets the girl, or against all odds he does the deed and wins the prize.

In our journey through existence, we encounter the material struggle of life as well as a parallel struggle to understand God in our lives. For some there is no fight or struggle, as they have no implied understanding or desire to know God or meet Him. For others, the adventure of life is all about struggle. The struggle to survive on this planet is inextricably bound with the spiritual struggle. "All the world is a stage," and we are all players in a cosmic drama that far transcends the foraging for food or the unlocking of a mystery in an Agatha Christie play.

So we embark on a command performance before the King; it is a mystery and a drama as we attempt to grapple with what we believe to be true and what we see laid out in the play before us. The struggle is to understand ourselves in the context of knowing God. It would be great to know all there is to know in the universe; however, as our societies change, and the nature of our understanding changes, we are confronted with the struggle to reconcile the differences. In our view of the cosmic play, we see ourselves as the heroes who will complete the mission against all odds. In athletics, only the fastest gets the prize. In this cosmic drama, many have that opportunity. There are many forms of theatre, and many roles in the play. Rather than accept our role as cast and set in a Shakespearean stage play, we will consider how we play our part and interact with the other pedestrians in a form of an improv or street theatre. *The Lord of the Rings* trilogy by J.R.R. Tolkien includes an excellent example of how we have been called to play a role in that cosmic play. It reflects the inner battle, the public actions, and the fellowship of a group as they unite to fight the good fight for a common cause.

And we shouldn't be here at all, if we'd known more about it before we started. But I suppose it's often that way. The brave things in the old tales and songs, Mr. Frodo: adventures, as I used to call them. I used to think that they were things the wonderful folk of the stories went out and looked for, because they wanted them, because they were exciting and life was a bit dull, a kind of sport, as you might say. But that's not the way of it with the tales that really mattered, or the ones that stay in the mind. Folk seem to have just landed in them, usually—their paths were laid that way, as you put it. But I expect they had lots of chances of turning back, only they didn't. And if they had, we shouldn't know, because they'd have been forgotten.[1]

As Sam stated to Frodo, the ones who turned back would be forgotten. The ones who finish the mystery, who press on to the end, will win the prize and the applause of the great King. So we, too, continue on the journey whether it is in the trenches of daily battle or on the stage of the cosmic play.

---

1   Tolkien, J. R. R. *The Two Towers*, pp. 320-321. George Allen & Unwin, 1954.

Section I:

THE PRIVATE BATTLE
& THEOLOGY

Hear, O Israel: The Lord our God, the Lord is one. Love the Lord your God with all your heart and with all your soul and with all your strength. These commandments that I give you today are to be on your hearts. Impress them on your children. Talk about them when you sit at home and when you walk along the road, when you lie down and when you get up. Tie them as symbols on our hands and bind them on your foreheads. Write them on the doorframes of your houses and on your gates.

The Shema
—Deuteronomy 6:4–9

Finally, be strong in the Lord and in his mighty power. Put on the full armor of God, so that you can take your stand against the devil's schemes. For our struggle is not against flesh and blood, but against the rulers, against the authorities, against the powers of this dark world and against the spiritual forces of evil in the heavenly realms. Therefore put on the full armor of God, so that when the day of evil comes, you may be able to stand your ground, and after you have done everything, to stand.

—Ephesians 6:10–13

VIGNETTE ONE

IT HAS BEEN THREE DAYS WITHOUT FOOD, AND A MINIMAL AMOUNT OF WATER or rest. Richard has had more than his share of time to contemplate life and his current circumstance, locked away and able to see nobody but his tormentors. They have been intent on getting him to confess to worshiping a pagan deity and to admit that his order has defied the Pope and the Church.

Richard joined the Knights Templar looking for adventure and to defend Christendom from the Muslim infidel. In his time with the Knights, he has never seen a Muslim! As it turns out, his tormentors are not the men of Islam, but the men of Prince Philip, King of France. The faces of the real enemy presented themselves within Christendom and not in the Holy Land.

During the time of relative peace between Islam and Christendom, the Knights Templar had moved their headquarters to Cyprus. They moved away from their base of support in Europe to be closer to the action, when it would occur again, in the Middle East. The move was meant to be strategic: to fulfill their orders to defend their portion of Christendom from Jerusalem to Acre. Unfortunately, with the current peace between Islam and Christendom, there was no tactical advantage in Cyprus and no visibility or support in Europe. It was expensive to mount an army and keep both men and horses equipped and fed. Early inscriptions would show two men mounted on a horse of the poor knights of the Order Templar. Over time, they were given gifts for their service and others entrusted them with their treasures here on earth for their safekeeping.

Prince Philip had his eye on those treasures entrusted to the "poor knights" for safekeeping. Now was the time for the prince to make his move. He rounded up all the knights of the order in France and kept them separated so they could not confer with or support each other. The king then sought to discredit the order with the Pope by extracting confessions from the knights. Once he had the confessions, he did not care what happened to the knights. This was not a holy war—he just wanted their land and their treasure.

Friday the 13th had taken on a whole new meaning since Richard was rounded up on Friday, October 13, 1307, along with all the other members of his order. Today, being Sunday, was a day of rest. The jailers and the jailed both got their rest. Richard was not tortured; however, neither did he get any food or fresh water. Today was a day for Richard to contemplate and reflect on his current lot in life. Would he succumb to the torture and current circumstances, or would he remain loyal and true to his order? Did it mean anything to just say "yes" to whatever they asked for? He would then be free to go and join another order. If they were really after the treasure, then it did not matter, since nothing of value remained in France. It had been shipped away to another location for safekeeping. The Knights had sworn their allegiance to God, the Pope, and Mary, and swore to protect the saints and their part of Christendom. They took very literally and seriously the role of God's warriors here on earth. They were here to defend the truth and God's Kingdom. Could defending the truth allow for a small lie?

The thought came to him that he could betray the order with his lips, but not his heart. He could say "yes" to his captors and not really mean it. Then Richard would be free to leave; however, if he ever recanted on his confession it would mean certain death. If he stayed here it would mean eventual death.

Richard's role in the cosmic play was clear. How he was to play that part was not as clear. Richard believed that God had provided a way of escape. He just had to find it.

★ ★ ★

Boray drove his Mercedes towards the hotel as he did at the start of every day. This day was not too much different. He reflected on the recent pronouncements from the White House, and he reflected on the teachings of the local imam. He remembered his second cousin's visit. His second cousin had told him many things about life in North America. He also reflected on what was beamed into his country every day by the American media. It did not seem that American values came even close to Islam.

Boray also reflected on his life. It was not perfect. No one, except the Prophet, could come close to the standard demanded by God. Despite praying faithfully each day and despite the fasting, giving, and religious observances, he felt emptiness and a lingering fear. There was a good feeling of being right and in observing tradition and routine. There was a great feeling of tradition and heritage in observing the practices that spanned well over forty generations. There was an inheritance, a blessing from God, which was traced for thousands of years to the first-born of Abraham. *Who is better in religion than he who surrenders his purpose to Allah while doing good, and follows the tradition of Abraham the upright? Allah (Himself) chose Abraham for a friend.*[2]

Yet there was a sense of entrapment. Not by any demands of submission to Islam, but more the entrapment of Boray's current lot in life. His life was one of constant struggle. It was also a life of great sacrifice— to make the pilgrimage to Mecca. Life was a struggle, yet he did not come close to the standard expected of God. Life was daily submitted to God and a daily sacrifice. The daily sacrifice was part of the whole struggle and holy war in Islam. All of Islam had struggled; in a sense, everyone was a mujahidin. The enemy, however, was a little less clear. Others may be close to God's standard, but certainly not the infidel—the great Satan of the United States would not come even close to His standard! How could they ever expect God to bless America?

There was also the struggle to survive in this economically hostile land. This land had been the heart of the mighty Ottoman Empire. Now it struggled between western values and culture and a solid heritage in Islam. The Americans, and before them the British, were taking the wealth of the land and in return trying to impose their political will. If their political system meant bringing the corruption and decaying moral standards of North America with it, then they could keep their democracy. Each day was a struggle to provide for his wife and two children. Each day was a struggle to submit his will to the will of God. Yet each day he feared

---

2   Qur'an, 4:125

he had missed the standard and there would be no way to atone or make up for his sins. Today was the chance to make one final sacrifice that would grant him safe passage to eternity and the promise that his family would be provided for. One simple sacrifice and the struggle would be finished.

Boray snapped back from his thoughts as the security guard at the gate from the street to the hotel entrance waved him through. Boray had done this job for years and was well known to the staff here; he went straight to the taxi queue.

This morning many western businessmen were queued up to attend a trade conference. They had come to Boray's country not out of respect for Islam or for the great history of the country. They had come in pursuit of profit and to worship their almighty dollar. As the doorman signaled, each taxi came up and one or two more men got in and headed off to their destination.

Now it was Boray's turn. He pulled up his car and as the door was opened, Boray closed the switch that sparked four hundred pounds of fuel and nitrates that sent seven men, and himself, to their eternal destination. The result of auto parts and body parts flying in every direction was to leave a large scar on the face of the hotel and a small mark in history.

Boray had submitted his will to make the ultimate witness and sacrifice, and in doing so he sent his final statement of faith to the world and the White House. In the same move, he provided for his family through the gifts of the community, and he was guaranteed to go on to his final reward. This was how he decided to end his part in this act of the cosmic play.

★ ★ ★

Ben's day started like any other. He got up early, stretched his arms and legs, and then it was out of his warm bed for a quick shave and shower. The shower couldn't drown out Ben's torturous cries as he spoke to God. "Why God, why do I have to struggle with an indifferent boss and a cold church congregation? Aren't we here to learn, grow, and serve you? We have dedicated our lives to your service and it is a struggle. No, it is more than a struggle. At times it seems to be arm to arm combat with the people in this church."

Kim, Ben's wife, could hear his cries from the shower as he continued to address God.

"Why do we have to struggle? What is the point of all this?" In the middle of Ben's speech, he considered that he should await God's reply. He washed his hair—there was no reply. As he rinsed his hair, he continued to expect an answer.

Ben struggled with the seeming complacency in his congregation. It appeared that they came to church not to worship the almighty God. It was a social club where people came, sang a few songs, expected to hear a nice talk, passed the plate, and then went home feeling good that they had done their religious duty. Church was not supposed to be like that! People were to come and encourage each other. Lives were to be transformed and God was to be glorified.

Then the answer came.

"The battle you fight is not your battle. The first life in that congregation to be transformed will be yours. The struggles you have are no more your struggles than when David fought Goliath. It was not Saul's war or David's battle. David understood that he was my soldier. Your struggles, like Joseph's, David's and Job's, are there that you may learn to serve me and that ultimately your life will honor me. I will give you the tools for battle. *For our struggle is not against flesh and blood, but against the rulers, against the authorities, against the powers of this dark world and against the spiritual forces of evil in the heavenly realms.*"[3]

As Ben stepped out of the shower and to the bedroom, he found a pile of ancient tools beside his bed. These were the weapons of spiritual war which included a belt, a sword, a shield, a helmet, and a breastplate. These were not the tools of a peasant farmer conscripted as soldier. These were the tools of a Roman Centurion—a professional soldier.

There is a biblical image of each person being a holy warrior equipped to stand firm against the enemy. The danger is that we would lash out at our human opponents as if they were the real enemy. While the struggle is with an enemy we cannot see, the visible tools reflect a power available to overcome forces both seen and unseen.

---

3   Ephesians 6:12

It starts with the belt of truth. Before Ben could try on any of the armor, his character would be prepared by laying the foundation with the truth. Truth is a character trait and foundation that would be refined through many trials. As Ben got dressed, he learned to clothe and secure himself with the truth. Then he donned the breastplate of righteousness. This was not a self-righteous attitude that would kill the spirit of others and lead him to destruction—it was a righteousness given to him, to be taken and worn. It was seen by many as an uprightness of character—a requirement not to neglect those principles of a holy warrior of God. Ben would prepare himself for the daily battle as those before him had done for many years by donning the tools for a holy war. Ultimately the warrior was made ready and strong not to attack but to protect the weak. He would be ready to fight the laziness and neglect of the congregation and to lead them into a personal battle of truth and righteousness in holy war. They would see the strength given to him by his personal preparations for battle and would be encouraged to follow his example and lead.

1. The Private Battle

WHAT DO RICHARD, BORAY, BEN AND THE REST OF US HAVE IN COMMON? IT is that we all wrestle or encounter struggles in life. The great divergence is in how we understand and handle that struggle. Everything could be viewed as a struggle from the time we get up in the morning until we go to bed at night. There are struggles as a parent. There are struggles in relationships. There are struggles at work. There are so many struggles in life! On reflection, a better word is the Arabic word Jihad. Here the word could translate into struggle; however, there is more history and a richer meaning to the word.

While we could associate Jihad with terrorists and bombing, it is also seen as a personal internal struggle. Ultimately it is a struggle not to succumb to the wild man within, but to reflect the image of God on the outside. Eventually it grows to become a corporate struggle where the people of God struggle to see His will done here on earth as it is in heaven. Some will mistake the corporate struggle to the extreme point of a holy war and promote killing the infidels and apostates—sending them to their eternal destiny in the name of God. However, the greater unseen struggle is that personal guerrilla war waged every day by believers against an enemy we cannot see or fight with the traditional tools of war.

On reflection, the battle and the struggle are waged on three fronts. The personal front is the internal war, the war rarely seen and seldom spoken; it is the struggle between my ears and my ribs for the supremacy of my being. It is the struggle to hold my thoughts captive and set them apart from the everyday noise that bombards us. It is that continuous civil war between the self-centered wickedness of my will and the desire to be transformed into the image and desires of God. The public war includes the struggles we have and that others can actually see, so we may ultimately have to acknowledge them. The public war is a Jihad of relationships at home, at school, and in the workplace. These battles are won and lost in our words and actions. The corporate war is where the community of faith bands together and seeks to fight the good fight to the honor of God. It is the corporate holy war that makes the headlines of newspapers; however, it is the battles won and lost on the internal front that determine the outcome on the public front. It is the personal battles fought on a billion fields every day that develop into the final outcome of the holy war.

The provision has been set for us to win that war. God is sovereign and will ultimately win it. The outcome is known and plans have already been made for the victory parade. That victory parade, if you can imagine it, will be like in the times of Rome, where the victors and their leader were at the head of the parade, with the spoils of war and the captives pulled along to be displayed and then dispatched. At issue, for me, is which side of the front are we on? My concern for all of the world's citizens is the apparent lack of struggle. For some the absence of struggle could mean victory. More likely it means capitulation in battle. Our apparent blessings have become substitutes for abiding in a relationship with God. We could find ourselves drifting away from God in the same way ancient Israel did. As they were carried off to Babylon, some of them woke up to the fact that they had not been in God's will. On reflection, it became His will for them to be taken away from the Promised Land. It was the negative result of countless personal and public battles that led Israel ultimately to lose favor with God and lose their land. Israel may have lost favor with God, but they had not lost the promise. Even in that struggle, God used His people during the rule of the Gentiles.

For Israel and the Jewish faith, God is a God of history. God is the creator and He is known through His interactions with His chosen people through time. God chose Abraham and in faith Abraham responded to God. God broke through the normal channels and called Abraham out of the comfort zone in his town to wander through what is now known as the Middle East. Abraham took God at His word and promise. There was the promise of an heir and the promise of a land for his heirs.

Life for Abraham was not easy. There were struggles on many fronts. Abraham had to deal with the personal and public disappointment of not yet having an heir. His servant would inherit his fortune. Despite being blessed with material wealth, Abraham had no one to continue his name.

There were struggles as he traveled from place to place. On more than one occasion, Abraham feared for his life and lied about his relationship with his wife. The first corporate battle recorded in the Bible followed some of the principles of holy war in Genesis 14 when Abraham rescued his nephew Lot. In the biblical account, he took no spoils and he gave an offering to the priest—King Melchizedek.

Generations later, Moses was called to lead his people from Egypt to the Promised Land. The battle with Pharaoh was not fought with the traditional weapons of war at the time. The great "I Am" fought the fight. The people of Israel took the spoils of war with them as they fled to cross the Red Sea. The people had to follow Moses, who—as instructed from God—was to lead the people in an unconventional spoiling of their Egyptian masters. For Israel to be victorious, they had to start by being obedient and follow the instructions given by Moses for the Passover. If a family did not follow the instructions to slay a lamb and paint the blood on the doorframe of their home, then the family would suffer the same fate as their Egyptian neighbors: the death of their firstborn. The Exodus outlines the people's struggle to understand and follow as well as their fickle faith in watching the arm of El Shaddai conquer the enemy. Exodus 12 to 15 outlines God's mighty works as He conquers the enemy. In Exodus 17 again we see that Israel defeated the Amalekites by the hand of God.

The year following the Exodus, the people of Israel became a distinct people. They were fed with manna from heaven six out of every seven days. Water came from a rock. They got tired of manna and were fed quail. Moses instructed them in how to craft the Tabernacle and the Ark of the Covenant. The wardrobe of the priests and the icons of worship distinguished them as people of the one true God. While some of the symbols may have been familiar to them from Egypt, the symbols were also distinct and separate from those of Egypt and the surrounding lands. They were tangible reminders that they were a people of God the Creator, and that He, not a cow, delivered them from their tormentors.

It was considered a good idea to send spies to see the land God had given them. Twelve spies, one from each tribe, were sent. The prospects there were great; however, the fear of "giants" in the land caused Israel to reject the land and the command to take it. They saw that the battles would be too big for them to overcome on their own. They failed to realize it was not their battle. Later, in Numbers 14, we see Israel defeated after they have realized the result of their rejection of God and His command to take the Promised Land. When they later decided to attack, they failed since they were not instructed by God. A principle to be gained by this observation is that holy war requires holy and faithful warriors, and holy war is made up of God's battles—not battles of our own choosing.

In declaring a holy war, God required all things set aside for Him to be His alone. This is found in Leviticus 27:28–29. What is set aside as holy and for God remains His. What is set aside for destruction cannot redeemed. This is echoed again in Deuteronomy 13:12–18 when a city in the Promised Land had gone astray and the people were required to gather the plunder and burn the town as a burnt offering to God. Deuteronomy 20 sets the parameters of holy war. There was an option to take prisoners and spare their lives. The purpose for the annihilation of the enemy is specified in verse 18:

> *Otherwise, they will teach you to follow all the detestable things they do in worshiping their gods, and you will sin against the Lord your God.*
> —Deuteronomy 20:18

The purpose for the sacrifice of the plunder and the death of the inhabitants was to keep the people of God holy. In a practical sense, there was also no one left to lay claim to the land of Israel's possession. When Israel left survivors, they became a thorn in their side.

In the book of Joshua, after forty years of wandering through the desert, we again see holy war. This time, Joshua takes the Promised Land following God's guidance through the Jordan and around Jericho to conquer the great walled city and the surrounding lands. In Joshua 6:18–20, the city of Jericho was dedicated to God by marching around its outer walls and sounding the ram's horn. With the exception of Rahab and her family, all of the occupants of the city and the city itself were to be destroyed.

Again, with unfaithfulness there was failure; with faithfulness to God's calling there was miraculous deliverance. There was failure in

Joshua's campaign. It was known as Achan's sin. Outlined in Joshua 7 is the story of what should have been another easy victory that went wrong. Later in the chapter it was identified that Achan had taken a robe, silver, and gold from the plunder of the previous campaign. No one had seen him do it. However, it was not a theft from a neighbor or a dead victim; it was a theft from God. Did God need the silver and gold? No, God required a disciplined and holy warrior to carry out His cause. At issue was that Achan's sin was not limited to just taking stuff; he had changed his focus and allegiance from his king to his own selfish desires.

While Joshua and Israel were successful in conquering the land, they renewed their covenant with God. Right after that time, there is recorded another point of failure known as the Gibeonite deception. The Gibeonites had heard about Joshua's success and knew Israel was headed their way, so they resorted to a ruse. They dressed themselves up in worn-out clothes, provided themselves with old and moldy food, and made their way to visit Joshua and the camp of Israel. When they met Joshua, they said, "We have come from a distant country and want to make a treaty with you."

The Israelites asked, "How can we trust you?"

The Gibeonites replied, "We are your servants and we have come from a long way. Check out our supplies."

The telling verse is in Joshua 9:14: *"The Israelites sampled their provisions but did not inquire of the Lord."*

Joshua then made a treaty with the Gibeonites, and then found out three days later they were neighbors living nearby. They could not do anything because they had made an oath before God. At issue was that Joshua and the leaders of Israel had trusted their own insight. The second lesson of holy war is to inquire of God!

After the initial conquest of the Promised Land, the people of Israel continued to expand their boundaries. While the people of Israel now had a home, the book of Judges documents their spiritual wandering and its consequences.

Not all the original inhabitants were driven from the land. They remained in the land and coexisted with Israel. Time after time, judges were raised up to call Israel back to God and to set them apart as a Holy

Kingdom and a Holy Priesthood among the nations. The Israelites wanted to be more like their neighbors and demanded a king. Holy war took on a new dimension in the books of Samuel as Saul was appointed King of Israel. Saul was God's ambassador to the nations. Saul, as the notional head of state and ambassador, should have followed the lead from his God and king.

Saul was successful on his first campaign. Later, the prophet Samuel, who had anointed Saul as king, came out to see Saul. Samuel asked Saul, "What is this bleating of sheep I hear?" Saul had violated a principle of holy war—it was the Lord's (God's). Saul had failed to follow instructions; whether it was to vanquish the king and his people or the destruction of the livestock. Ultimately, Saul lost the right to be king.

In another of Saul's battles, the Philistines made the practical proposition of sending the best men to act as a proxy for the entire armies. David happened to be around when he heard Goliath's proposal, and he understood that Goliath's challenge was against Israel and their God. David also understood it was not Saul's battle—it was God's. God had already equipped David with the tools he needed for the battle. These were not the traditional tools of swords and shield—those would come later. On that famous day, David went out with the equipment and experience that had already proven successful. David also went out knowing he was on stage and was performing for and on behalf of his king, the Lord God Almighty.

As everyone knows from the story of David and Goliath, David was successful. There was celebration throughout all Israel! The people sang that Saul had slain his thousands, but David had slain his ten thousands. David eventually went on to become King of Judah and all of Israel. His ascendancy to the throne was not without struggle.

After the reign of David and his son Solomon, Israel again lost its way. In this time, the people of God looked forward to the Day of the Lord. This was a day when God would reestablish Israel to its former glory by bringing a Savior to liberate His people from those who oppressed them from every border. The prophet Amos crossed the border to his brothers in Israel to declare that the Day of the Lord would not be good news for the people of Israel. God demanded that His people be a people of justice and mercy and not oppress the poor or deal unfairly. The result would be that the Kingdom of Israel would be shredded and only a remnant of the former kingdom would remain.

Holy war has a purpose. The purpose in the Old Testament was for God's people to take the land and establish it as an embassy for the Kingdom of God. As the people of God lost sight of their purpose, they also lost their land and were taken captive first by the Assyrians, then by the Babylonians, and then by the Persians. As the people of God became the people of the book and a people of prayer, they gained back their land, their city, and the temple again as an embassy to the nations.

During the period of the Maccabees, we have the introduction of the original mid-east terrorist! The Zealots, in their determination to regain the homeland and rid themselves of Greek cultural influences, would murder sympathizers of their Greek rulers. While deception and deceit were documented earlier, the Maccabees took these strategies to new levels, and were elevated in stature to hero status in the historical books of the Maccabees. The Greeks were eventually replaced by the Romans.

When Jesus the Christ came, He was declared the Son of Man, the Son of David, and the Son of God. His claim to be the Son of David was proven by taking His lineage on both His mother's and supposedly His father's sides and tracing it back to the glory days of King David. It was a political title. The claim was to the lineage of King David. If He was the son of David, they would look to Him as the Messiah, as a political and military leader who would free Israel from the shackles of the oppression of Rome.

Among His band of disciples, Jesus included one of the original mid-east terrorists—Simon the Zealot. The zealots were looking to overthrow the occupation of Rome and reestablish God's kingdom in Israel; however, Jesus made it clear that His kingdom was not of this world. Jesus also took the title of Son of Man. During the triumphal entry (in the last week of his earthly life), He came riding into Jerusalem on a young colt—not a stallion. Jesus preached the coming of the kingdom of God and the gospel of peace. It was not a military truce or a political solution. It was not a kingdom that would overtake Rome—it was a kingdom that would permeate Rome. In this case, holy war took on a new meaning! It was not traditional armed combat. The weapons of the day were merely props for a much bigger play. Jesus took Israel's history and the prophets and refreshed the entire meaning of Scripture. We are reminded that there were times when Israel was called not to fight or defend the land. The prophet Jeremiah called on his countrymen to give it up to the pagans, for this was in God's plan. Jesus declared, *"All who draw the sword will die by the sword"* (Matthew 26:52). The real battle is the final battle outlined in Scripture. The act of crucifying Jesus Christ at the time was seen as a tragedy; however, the daily, weekly, monthly, and annual sacrifices of the Old Testament would be replaced by His one sacrifice for all.

As we plot the trend in events and understanding of the Bible, we see a trend from conversion by the sword to a time when we will all worship God in spirit and truth. After the sacrifice of Christ on the cross, the Kingdom of Heaven grew within the empire of Rome like the mustard seed. The persecution of the believers of the way, later to be called Christians, led to the spread of the gospel of the Kingdom of God throughout the entire Roman Empire and beyond. This kingdom was growing by the edge of the sword, but not the way the original Zealots thought it would. The believers were on the wrong end of the sword.

At the same time, Judaism was also getting hit on two sides. First a rabbi, Saul of Tarsus, who worked to defeat this Jewish sect that had followed Jesus of Nazareth, had converted to become a follower and a member of the way. It was purported that he had told fellow Jews they did not have to follow the rituals as set out in the law. Secondly, the Zealots had taken matters into their own hands and started a rebellion that would last years until the fall of Jerusalem and the final destruction of the temple in AD 70. The Jewish people had looked for a Messiah who would deliver them from their political tormentors. The result at that time was the physical reality of the end of the sacrificial system and the fulfillment of the prophecy, made forty years earlier, that the temple would be destroyed. The people of God would have to worship the God Almighty only in spirit and in truth, yet there was still the reality of a holy people under the political tyranny of Rome.

Judaism and Christianity would be under the thumb of Rome until the Edict of Milan in 313. The Edict was a peace treaty to the Church, and it marked the start of the two-way assimilation of Roman culture into the Church and the Church's values into Roman culture.

Rome was not going to spend its energies fighting the Church within its boundaries. It needed its resources to fight the barbarians on the frontiers. While there was short-term relief for the Church, life wasn't any better for Judaism. Now the head of state was involved in theological issues in which he was not trained. Whether Constantine treated Christianity as a good luck charm, or whether he needed another god to fight the other gods, or whether he was indeed a true believer, the debate will continue as long as there are people to contemplate the results of his actions. Over time, Christian fortunes would start to reflect the fortunes of the host state. With the split of the Roman Empire came the split in the Church. With the demise of the Western Roman Empire came the ascendancy of the Roman Catholic Church. The Pope, as the head of the Church on earth, was the head of state of God's Kingdom on Earth. He was the lead administrator, ambassador, and effectively the head of state. A church doctrine of just war was developed. Over time, the Church started to look like the other nations. The national armies would be used as well as three military orders established within the Roman Catholic Church to carry on and defend its affairs. The Church had strayed very far from the teachings of Jesus. The military orders now employed the sword as representatives of a nation supposedly built on the teachings of Jesus Christ—who had said "he who lives by the sword dies by the sword."

Six hundred years after Jesus Christ walked the earth, parallel to the political rise and moral decline of the Roman Catholic Church, Mohammed, a prophet—not a messiah—was calling his people away from their pagan rituals back to the worship of the one true God. In his declarations, later preserved in the Quran, he called his people to be the *mujahidin,* which are the holy warriors. They are the ones who prepare physically, mentally, and emotionally for a holy war. Theirs is the life of discipline for the final goal. When I read about the *mujahidin* and Islam, I was impressed by their discipline to find God and serve him. Islam is about submission. There are five basic pillars of submission common to all of Islam:

1. **Shahada** – Proclamation of the one God Allah
2. **Salah** – Prayer five times a day
3. **Zakat** – To purify or cleanse through the giving of alms
4. **Sawm** – The fast of Ramadan
5. **Hajj** – The pilgrimage to Mecca

The disciplines of Islam were borne out of struggle. Unlike current western Christianity, where we tend to compartmentalize our lives, Islam claims to be an all-encompassing system which currently also proscribes culture and government. History and culture come as a package with the religious beliefs. In modern western Christianity, there is a separation between church and state. This is mostly in reaction to the abuses of the past. The Crusades were seen as a holy war against Islam. Christendom was not prepared militarily or spiritually to initiate the Crusades. From our current perspective, it was a disaster for all sides. We had very unchristian men do the most ungodly things in the name of Christendom. It did not reflect the values of Christ, so it was also a failure in reflecting Christian values. We had children march out on the Children's Crusade, only to be taken or to die on the way to the Holy Land. So it was a failure on a spiritual, political, and military level. What we had then, and still have today, are men and women calling on the name of God, or doing actions on behalf of God, with little or no thought or reflection of God.

For some today, the Crusades continue. There is still a holy war and some see themselves as holy warriors prepared to kill or die for the cause. Today, we don't need more political battles or even traditional holy wars. What is needed is an army of true holy warriors. In the tradition of holy war, God called up the enemies of Israel to bring them back to Him. The Babylonian captivity was a result of the apostasy of the Jewish state and the corruption of justice. With the rise of Christianity and what was left of the Roman Empire becoming Christian came the ascendancy of the power of the Roman Catholic Church and the rise of corruption within that organization. The Dark Ages is an apt description for the period when the Church and corruption ruled supreme. While in that time there were enlightened Popes, more often than not the period of church history was characterized by struggles over structure and power. Perhaps, like Babylon, God raised the Islamic Empire to call Christians and Jews (people of the book) back to Him.

If that is the case, then perhaps the current Islamic uprising should not be viewed with the current modern western rational mindset. What is needed is not more "homeland security." What is needed is for nations and individuals to turn from our current self-centered, narcissistic mindset—to look upward and outward. Rather than a crusade against terrorists and freedom fighters, the first crusade needs to be to demolish the enemy strongholds within our minds and culture. In light of our understanding of the history of holy war and current events, Islam's public Jihad is a call to Christians and Jews, both nominal and committed, back to God. We are to become true people of the book. As a Christian, I may not struggle to find God; I struggle to serve God and understand Him. The struggle is not what is God, but who is God. Ultimately the who goes beyond facts and information and extends to a personal relationship with a personal God. The call to arms is a call to each and every one of us to be *mujahidin* and to arm ourselves with the spiritual weapons of holy war and to reflect on our understanding of God, who is our commander in chief.

2. THEOLOGY

THEOLOGY IS THE STUDY OF GOD. THIS BRIEF REFLECTION HERE IS NOT MEANT to be a full history of philosophical and theological thought. The study of God, or our understanding of God, comes through numerous paths. Depending on the path we choose, it may lead to a different understanding of God. This is far different from the popular thought that all roads lead to Rome or that all religions lead to the same God. Clearly Judaism, Christianity, and Islam all refer to the same God of Abraham; however, their understanding of the nature of God differs.

What's in a name? One God, one name: Allah. In a mid-eastern sense, to name was to have control or dominion over the person or thing named. In Genesis 1, when God created the light and named it day and night, it meant He had dominion over the day and night. In Genesis 2, when Adam named the animals, it was his first act of care or dominion over the animals. A name also represented an attribute of a person. As an example, in 1 Samuel David encountered a man named Nabal, meaning "fool." In fact, Nabal acted foolishly. When God confronted Moses at the burning bush and asked him to go on His behalf, Moses asked God's name. If Moses knew the name of God, he could use it in terms of their relationship. At that time there were many gods. Surely the Egyptians would want to know which god Moses represented and whether this god was worth listening to. There was a lot of meaning wrapped up in the name of God. God's answer was to tell Pharaoh and the Israelites that the great "I Am" sent him. We are not to know the name of God; however, there are many titles for God. The Tetragrammaton is the technical term for the four letters in the Hebrew alphabet that stand for God's name. We may guess, but we don't really know how to say it! There are other names in the Bible given for God. Another name for God the creator is Elohim. Each name or title is a reflection of our understanding of the attributes of God. Reflecting on each name gives us a bigger picture of God. Our choice of names reflects, to some degree, our theology. The

Man Upstairs or Abba are different titles and reflect different views on God. The Man Upstairs is a detached view of God—Abba, or father, reflects a very personal attachment and relationship with God.

As we contemplate life and all of its struggles, it is our understanding of God that becomes the most important factor in determining the outcome of those struggles. What we think of, or how we consider God, impacts how we think about the rest of life, our life philosophy, and how we should act. Is how I came to be in this point of my life a matter or pure luck, choice on my part, or divine providence? We can act as if there is no tomorrow and no consequences for our actions, if we do not believe we are responsible to a god who created the world and everything within it. Our understanding of God also determines what we believe happens after we die. If there is no God, no supreme being, and no design in creation, we could expect there will be no consequences for our actions. We may go through this path many times until we attain a state of Nirvana, we may go through it once with eternal consequences, or we may just go through it once. If we go through this place just once with no consequences, what is the point in being a good person?

We may also have some anthropocentric views of God. An anthropocentric view puts man in the center of the universe. When we're in the middle, we see God as a cosmic bellhop created to fulfill our wishes. If we do a bunch of good things, He will give us everything we ask. Some may choose to pray to their god with some formula of understanding that those prayers will produce certain results for them. In some cases we do not even need to pray. All we need to do is unleash the higher power within to think and grow rich.

Anthropomorphism attributes human qualities to non-human entities. Anthropomorphism gives Mickey Mouse and Donald Duck their human attributes. It also gives us the term "the arm of God." In the same way the Greeks gave their gods human qualities, in many aspects their gods were not much different than their creators. An anthropomorphic and anthropocentric point of view puts man, not God, in the middle. The danger in reflecting on an anthropomorphic view of God is that He cannot be much more than we can attribute, and so He is in the same category as Mickey Mouse or the gods of Greek myths. From this perspective, the concept of god might be good for the kids, but the myths are of no help when we face our daily struggles. The result is that we can drop off our kids at Sunday school to learn the Bible stories. We then feel that the stories are not much more value beyond Sunday school when the pressures of real life come, because our view of God is no bigger than ourselves. So God is there in Sunday school, but a relationship with God gets crowded out by our concerns for real life.

Other concepts of God can stretch beyond the here and now. They stretch the known boundaries of the planet to an expansive universe and eternity. God the creator exists outside of His creation. He is not dependent on creation any more than J.S. Bach was dependent on his compositions. Many will acknowledge the existence of God or a "supreme being" for creation as we know it; however, they will also posit that God, like Bach, is no longer active in his composition. The universe as we know it has rules which we can determine through study. In the same way, I can learn something about Johann Sebastian Bach by studying *The Art of Fugue*. I could learn about him and his composition; however, I would not have a complete picture of the composer by just studying his work. It is the same with our understanding of God. We cannot get a complete understanding of God by studying His creation. We can learn a lot about God through His creation. We can find order within the universe; however, we cannot learn everything about God from within His creation any more than studying *The Art of Fugue* or the *Brandenburg Concertos* would give us a complete picture of Bach. We could come to the same conclusion as Antony Flew, who determined that there is a God, a supreme being, involved in creation, but from his observations, he could not say if that supreme being was the God of the Old or New Testaments. Over and above the compositions, we would need an autobiography of the creator to get a better understanding of God and our position in His creation.

Pre-Reformation theology was based on tradition and an allegorical approach to scriptures. The church traditions and teaching became more important and scriptures were referenced in support of their teaching. Systems of thought were built up to sustain the current power structures, and spiritual life died on the inside. With the sparks of new theological thought and life coming from the protesters came the renewal of theological thought. Eventually the renewal came from within and spawned the Protestant movement and the Reformation.

During the Reformation, Reformed theologians developed their five pillars, or the five *Solas*, of reformed theology. This was in reaction to the traditional theological thought of the Catholic Church at the time. The five *Solas* are:

1. **Sola Scriptura** – Only through Scripture. The Bible, not the traditional teachings of the Catholic Church, has authority over our thoughts and lives.
2. **Soli Deo Gloria** – Glory only to God.
3. **Sola Christo** – Salvation only through the work of Jesus Christ.
4. **Sola Gratia** – Only by grace—Salvation is not a matter of works or buying your salvation.
5. **Sola Fide** – Only by faith—Salvation and justification is by faith alone.

Salvation and redemption are a work of faith by grace alone, not of any work on our part. That work was done through Jesus Christ, and the nature of His work is described through the Scriptures. All of this is for the glory of God alone. Salvation cannot be earned or purchased. During the pre-Reformation period, the medieval church tried to stamp out those embers of life. There was a new battle and the church had engaged in the traditional methods of battle to fight a spiritual war. The leaders and followers of the Protestant movement took the words of Paul to heart as they again became witnesses (*martur* in Greek) for their beliefs.

In Ephesians 6:10–18, Paul exhorts us to be strong *"in the Lord and in His mighty power."* It is not our war, and we cannot win the war in our own power. While there were soldiers dispatched with swords and shields, the fight was not against flesh and blood. The traditional weapons of warfare were useless in this cosmic battle. This is a story of greater size and impact than any Star Wars episode. In equipping armies for holy war, we need holy warriors equipped with the appropriate weapons of war. There is a saying, don't bring a knife to a gun fight. The same holds true here. Our talents in persuasion are useless against Satan's wiles. Understanding the latest philosophies gives us an edge in debate; however, some of our natural strengths can be turned into weakness as we succumb to pride and envy.

We "know" things—but do not take the time to live that knowledge. As a society, we are so busy trying to achieve all the goals we have set ahead of us with no time to reflect. So we need the interior disciplines. The disciplines may be seen as a duty or a drudgery; however, in our desire to know about God, and ultimately to know Him, the personal disciplines transform us and so are also transformed from duty to become our delight. By exercising the personal disciplines, we become fit for spiritual battle. Each faith will make claims to holy ground, to a heritage, and to know God. While the Jewish people can claim a heritage of Abraham, Isaac, and Jacob (Israel), Islam claims its heritage through Abraham and Ishmael. As for Christians, their claim is that they are the adopted sons of God through their faith in Jesus Christ. To start to learn about God and His mighty deeds requires that you read His Word with a hope of understanding the Word as it was written and as it applies to us today. Our theology is forged during the time we read and reflect on the nature of God. The hope is that as we reflect on God, and the nature of God, our thoughts are inspired and our lives are transformed to be a holy people, holy witnesses, or holy warriors for God. As holy warriors, are we called to a full-scale holy war, or will we be trained to be UN Peacekeepers? In preparation for holy war, you need to prepare as a soldier and sharpen the sword. So our theology is no longer a book that sits collecting dust on a shelf.

The first discipline to explore relates to books and the source for life-changing theology: it is in reading the scriptures.

3. READ

SCRIPTURE—SHARPENING YOUR SWORD TO KNOW GOD IS TO READ HIS WORD.
There are many books about God; however, few books can claim divine
authorship. Among the few major books that make the claim of divine
authorship are the Bible and the Quran.

The Bible, as it was originally written, is a collection of letters and
books that over time have stood the test of the authority of God. The
two major divisions are the Old Testament and the New Testament. The
Bible was written by forty individuals over two thousand years and bears
the message and imprint of God acting in the life of His creation. God is
a historical god. He acted in the beginning and throughout history, and
the Bible is a written testament to that.

The Quran in its entirety was written by one man, Mohammad.
Technically, Mohammad did not write the Quran. He heard and held
the word, then he recited it and it was transcribed by some of his followers. In his writing, Mohammad points back to the first five books of the
Bible, the Psalms, and the Gospels. His writings attest to the God of creation, and a God of judgment. Two of Islam's messages include that the
people of Israel corrupted the original message of God, so Mohammad
was called to set the record straight. Mohammad called his people away
from their current pagan rituals to worship the one true God—the God
of Abraham. The Quran also claims to be the progressive revelation of
God's will. Interpretation of the Quran requires an understanding that
some of its earlier teachings have been superseded by later writings con-
tained in the same volume. From a western mindset, it does not help that
the Quran is not organized in a "logical" chronological progression.

Hermeneutics is the discipline of interpretation. It is typically used
in the context of determining the principles for understanding the Bible.
The entire Bible, Old Testament and New, was given to us and is useful
for training that we may be thoroughly equipped for every good work.

So as you approach Scripture, the hermeneutic is the philosophy of how you treat the text before you.

At first glance it may be difficult to understand how Numbers 26 or 1 Chronicles 4 may be applicable to our lives. So while we may have the tendency to skim through portions of the Bible, a second glace and some additional insight may yield material for one or two books. The book *The Prayer of Jabez* was based on an exposition of a few verses of 1 Chronicles 4.

Part of preparing for battle is to know your weapons. The first discipline for a holy warrior is to know God's word. The best way to begin is to just start reading it. To sharpen the sword, start by reading one or two portions a day. Start by reading a Psalm from the Old Testament each day, and then start reading the Gospel of Luke.

A foundational understanding is that the Bible can be understood, and is inspired, regardless of the language you use to read it. There is no secret code. Early theologians did think there was a secret code, and their interpretation was by allegory. In reaction to that idea, the reformers invoked Sola Scriptura where the code and the message become apparent by merely reading the word, and authority is solely with the word of God. Some people will treat only the King James or another version of the Bible as authoritative, when in fact the Bible was originally written in Hebrew, Aramaic, and Greek. The point is that you do not have to be a Greek or Hebrew scholar to understand the principles and message of the Bible. The strength of the Bible, as the written word of God, is that it cuts through all cultural and language barriers. The strength of Scripture is that when someone reads the Bible it can speak to them in their language and their circumstances.

Our primary job as we approach Scripture is to determine a hermeneutic, or philosophy of interpretation. How we approach Scripture will determine what we get out of it. We can approach it like a scientific textbook, a historical record, poetry, case law, a user guide, or life's blueprint. How you consider it, including your thoughts on its authorship, will determine how you read and interpret it. You could take every word literally. That works well for "Thou shalt not kill," or "Honor your parents." It does not work well if you take arbitrary portions of Scripture and string them together. The classic example of this is to open the Bible at random and have your finger land on Matthew 27:5, *"Judas threw the money into the temple and left. Then he went away and hanged himself."* You may consider that passage weird and conclude that it does not apply to you. So you repeat the exercise and your finger lands on, *"Jesus told him, 'Go and do likewise'"* (Luke 10:37b). If you needed any further encouragement, you might try the exercise again and your finger would land on, *"What you are about to do, do quickly"* (John 13:27). Taken in the extreme, using a literal interpretation and snatching excerpts from Scripture is like frantically flipping through an automotive repair manual looking for answers when you realize that your car won't start. On reflection, it would have been better to have worked through the manual to gain a basic understanding of the contents before you encountered the emergency.

The Bible is not an automotive repair manual; neither is it purely a blueprint. Let us review a few methods of reading:

- literal
- metaphorical
- allegorical
- historical grammatical

A literal view is that the words are to be taken exactly as written. If it says "Do not kill," then you do not kill. If it says "An eye for an eye and tooth for a tooth," then you can take your revenge up to a certain limit. The literal view, in all cases, is not enough. We recognize that when Scripture (Psalm 1) paints the picture of the righteous man as a tree planted by the river, he is not literally a tree planted by the river. In Matthew 7, when Jesus speaks about the wise man who built his house on the rock as opposed to the foolish man who built his house on the sand, it is not an instruction in carpentry. It's a metaphor for the spiritual foundation we build our life upon. These examples are obvious; other cases are not as obvious. In earlier times, including up to today, some will find that neither a literal nor a metaphorical approach is helpful in understanding some passages of Scripture.

The allegorical approach expands the use of metaphor to another level, removing the reader one more level from the literal meaning of the words. The danger with this approach is when you need a special knowledge or interpretation. The major concern is when the interpretation of a passage denies or takes away from the literal meaning of the passage.

Discussions on difficult topics like the existence of Hell and the nature of Hell may lead to using an allegorical approach to Scripture. A literal view would say there is a place of continual burning or fire and brimstone as appealing as the garbage dump outside Jerusalem thousands of years ago. A metaphorical view would hold that there is a place and it is as terrible as that garbage dump and the effect of being there would be like being continually consumed, but never finished, in the lake of burning fire; however, it may not be actually a burning lake of sulphur. An allegorical approach leaves wide open what Hell is really like and whether people are destined to spend eternity there or whether the torture, or separation from God, would simply seem like eternity. The allegory gets extended and embellished with many facets of Hell that we do not see in Scripture. It was this view, an allegorical interpretation, which was the foundation for purgatory. It comes from that hermeneutic and the understanding that God is a God of justice and love and that He would not want to see anyone perish. So a method of escape was designed through purgatory. During the medieval period, if you wanted your relatives to spend less time in that bad place you could buy an indulgence. The indulgence served two purposes: one was a partial reduction of punishment in purgatory granted by the Church, and the second was that money from the sales of the indulgences funded some excellent artwork and architecture. I cannot find any reference to a "get out of jail free" card or the Roman Catholic Church's indulgence in Scripture. An alternate allegorical approach may also allow for a punishment that seems like eternity but may end in annihilation. The danger in the allegorical view of Scripture is that it treats Scripture as secondary to the wishes of the interpreter.

In the historical grammatical method of interpretation, the scriptural text must be understood in its historical context and in its literary style. As an example, the Book of Revelation belongs to a certain literary genre. So it must be treated and understood in that language and context. It is not historical like the books of Samuel and Kings in the Old Testament. Our understanding of the Gospel of Matthew is enhanced when we realize the account was written by a Jewish tax collector. The original gospel may have been transcribed in Hebrew and later translated into Greek. Having an understanding of the time it was written, and the writer, enhances our understanding. This means we start out by taking the words in their most normal meaning. You take the words as they were originally written and apply them in their normal context. In the example of "Thou shalt not kill," it is obvious. In the case of the house on the sand, it is a metaphor. In the case of Jesus saying it is easier for a camel to go through an eye of a needle, He is using hyperbole common for the time and place. If He had been in another part of the world, it could be that we would say it would be easier for an elephant or horse to go through the eye of a needle than for a rich man to enter the gates of heaven. Does this mean the rich will not go to heaven? No, but it will be incredibly hard for them on their own merit. Why is that?

In the context of the proverb, Jesus was dealing with a rich young man (Matthew 19:16–29). The rich man had everything and asked Jesus what he must do to get eternal life. During the discussion, Jesus said, *"If you want to be perfect, go, sell your possessions and give to the poor, and you will have treasure in heaven. Then come, follow me"* (Matthew 19:21). Saddened by the thought of losing all his wealth, the rich man left Jesus. I do not think he followed Jesus' prescription. When we experience the good life and say that this is as good as it gets, there is no hope for a better tomorrow. So it would be extremely difficult for a rich person to hope, to long for, to crave, to yearn for a better place in heaven. The other thing to note is that when Jesus listed the commandments that the young man had not broken, "Thou shalt not covet" was not included. This guy was in love with the current material world. The other amazing thing in this context was that the general wisdom of the time was that God had blessed the rich man. Having wealth was seen as a reflection of God's blessing on your wisdom and work. So the disciples should have wondered, if a rich man can't get in to heaven, who can? The issue was that no one can get into heaven by their own efforts, but all things are possible with God. In the above context, it would be impossible for someone to go to heaven—just as it would be for a camel to go through the eye of the needle. Also in that context, we are to understand that with God all things are possible.

Our hermeneutic method should answer three things. The words can mean many things to many people, so the first thing to determine is what Scripture says. From a literal approach, we should know what those words say. It helps to understand the time and thought patterns when the words were written. The second thing to understand is the impact of those words in their historical setting. For Paul to write, *"There is neither Jew nor Gentile, neither slave nor free, nor is there male and female, for you are all one in Christ Jesus"* (Galatians 3:28) in the time of Rome was a revolutionary idea. Romans were at the top of the social order and slaves were not even considered part of that order. Slaves were property in the Roman era, in the same way we treat farm animals today. So when Paul dictated those words, it was revolutionary to consider that by the work of God all people would be equal in His kingdom.

The third aspect for our hermeneutic method to determine is the dynamic equivalent for today. That may mean determining who the slaves and free are today. What is the dynamic equivalent of "neither Jew nor Gentile"? Paul was writing his letter to the Galatians in the context of people saying they were better Christians because they were keeping the old Jewish customs. Whether your heritage was Jewish and you kept all the laws, or you were Greek and a new convert to Christianity, you were equal. We could take that one phrase and use it to say Paul accepted slavery. Given that he put slave and free on the same level, would that be a fair interpretation? Sometimes we need to work hard to find the equivalent of today's slaves—the downcast and the downtrodden. We need to wrestle with determining who the oppressed are and what we are called to do in a practical sense in our current context.

A simpler example could be found in the much-quoted Exodus 21:24: *"Eye for eye, tooth for tooth…"* What do the words actually say? What does it mean in an historical context? It is a primary directive of justice that puts limits on the level of redress for damages.

If we took the passage in a strict literal context then, quoting from *Fiddler on the Roof*, the country would be "blind and toothless." At the time the biblical imperative was given, it would have been common to inflict punitive damages to ensure the aggressor or trespasser did not do the action again. If you were responsible for one of my sheep dying, then I would go and take or kill three of your sheep. This appears to be like our current process of civil litigation—where we are suing everyone else for incredible sums of money. In this context, redress was limited to replacing just what was broken and no more. In a broader context, we can plot the line of limiting redress and revenge and move to the New Testament ethic of turning the other cheek. So quoting "eye for eye" as a basis for revenge would be inappropriate, given that it was meant to limit redress and that the ultimate imperative is to turn the other cheek and forgive the aggressor. If we read the Bible in total and apply our hermeneutic, that verse is not a command that we should take revenge—it is a command to limit revenge and, reading further to a New Testament ethic, we are encouraged not to seek revenge at all, but to turn the other cheek.

The hermeneutic of the Quran indicates that only the original Arabic version is holy. The true message, poetry, and flow of the Quran are only clearly evident in the original language. Various translations of the Quran abound; however, only the original language version is considered authoritative. The Quran looks back to the Old Testament and recites the events with a different worldview. If I read the Quran from cover to cover as I would read the Bible, it does not follow in the same way chronologically. I cannot plot the same developing trends of theological thought. Some of the latest writings are actually organized earlier in the book. There are many passages and references about God, Ibrahim (Abraham), Moses and Isa (Jesus), as well as people of the book. There are passages that directly address and confront the beliefs of Christians and Jews. In some cases there is a discrepancy in the understanding of an event between the Bible and the Quran. In one case—the crucifixion of Jesus—the Quran holds Jesus as a prophet and accepts the virgin birth and the event of the crucifixion; however, it does not allow that Jesus actually died on the cross. If Jesus actually died on the cross—that would be seen as a disaster; however, Islam does anticipate the victorious return of Christ as the Messiah. If we performed the typical rational comparison of the Bible and the Quran with cross-references, you would see many points of agreement; however, you cannot conclude that they both say the same thing! As the Quran points back to the Bible, it reaffirms the validity of the Bible, and uses that affirmation to also affirm the words from Mohammed.

How do we sharpen the sword and approach Scripture? We have to be careful in our methodology. The Bible is not a scientific textbook. Neither is it a mystery novel. As our hermeneutic will color how we read it, we also have to be aware of the language used. The meaning of words can change over time, so we have to be aware of how we apply the correct meaning to the word in the particular scriptural context. In that case, if you were to read the King James Version of the Bible, you would also have to understand the English used at the time of the translation as well as understand the context. A good modern translation would find the dynamic equivalent of the words in the context of the time. So it becomes our first priority to read the Bible, understand the general truths, and apply them to our situation.

4. REFUSE

THE SECOND KEY WORD FOR PERSONAL DISCIPLINE IS REFUSE. FASTING IS NOT a popular concept in our fast food culture! Western society is built upon instant gratification, overnight delivery, immediate downloads, and instant fulfillment. Then, even when we have enough, we want more! The result is that as a society we have become impatient, overindulgent, slothful, and overweight.

We are told there are many health benefits to fasting. Some will fast purely for personal health reasons. Fasting in a spiritual sense goes far beyond any health benefit or just refusing food for a day or a week. The intent of the fast is to get serious about our relationship with God. To forego food, the time preparing it, and the time consuming it, and free up your time to focus on God. A biblical fast is not a hunger strike! It is not intended to demand our way—the intent is to allocate our time and thoughts on seeking the center of God's will.

> *When you fast, do not look somber as the hypocrites do, for they disfigure their faces to show others they are fasting. Truly I tell you, they have received their reward in full. But when you fast, put oil on your head and wash your face, so that it will not be obvious to others that you are fasting, but only to your Father, who is unseen; and your Father, who sees what is done in secret, will reward you.*
>
> —Matthew 6:16–18

In the above passage, the religious people of the time had shifted the focus of the fast from God to themselves. By announcing their fast to everyone by their clothes and actions, they were putting themselves at the center of attention. Leviticus 16:29–31 describes the fast for the special day of atonement. It was one day set aside where no work was to be performed and you were to deny yourself. This was the one time a year set aside to commemorate the forgiveness of sins. It was a very public holy day. Over time, the fast became a weekly ritual. A practical fast in our western working world may mean allocating the day to discerning God's will for my life. That day would start with reading Scripture and prayer. It would then mean setting aside breakfast to spend more time reading and reflecting before continuing on to work. A strict definition of a fast would mean you would just have water; however, if we do not want to bring attention to ourselves we would have water and may join our colleagues at work either over tea or coffee at break time and lunch. In fact, I would still bring a visible sign of lunch; however, it would not be consumed. The time normally spent eating lunch, reading the paper, or idly chatting with friends would be traded for a quiet time of further reading, reflection, and prayer at my workplace. As the day goes on, my body makes me aware of the fast. At this point it becomes a discipline not to eat food. It also becomes a reminder that I have dedicated the day to earnestly seeking God's will in my life. The goal of the fast is not to make others see that I am more spiritual. If anything, they may think it is weird! The point is not to bring attention to ourselves. It is not to be legalistic in following the fast. At issue is to turn our focus on what God desires of us and not what we demand and expect from God. The goal of the fast is to sharpen our focus and determination to be servants and soldiers of the most High King. The center of the fast is God; everything else becomes secondary.

The discipline of fasting shows the seriousness of our commitment. Fasting is not a requirement to believe in God, but it does help us to focus on our relationship with Him. As an athlete prepares for the game, a soldier for the battle, or a musician for the concert, we have to put aside a few things so we can focus on and prepare for the future event. In the same way, fasting allows us to refuse a few things and put aside a few things so that our time and mental focus can be on our relationship with God. It is a physical reinforcement of our desire to know God and to serve Him.

Sometimes we do not need to pray or fast to know God's will. We know God's will and we just need to do it! The following passage, found in Isaiah 58:1–9a, indicates what God desires in the fast. It would be hypocritical to show off to others that we are fasting and then oppress those around us. More than fasting or sacrifices, God desires that we exercise justice.

"Shout it aloud, do not hold back.
Raise your voice like a trumpet.
Declare to my people their rebellion
and to the descendants of Jacob their sins.
For day after day they seek me out;
they seem eager to know my ways,
as if they were a nation that does what is right
and has not forsaken the commands of its God.
They ask me for just decisions
and seem eager for God to come near them.
'Why have we fasted,' they say,
'and you have not seen it?
Why have we humbled ourselves,
and you have not noticed?'

"Yet on the day of your fasting, you do as you please
and exploit all your workers.
Your fasting ends in quarreling and strife,
and in striking each other with wicked fists.
You cannot fast as you do today
and expect your voice to be heard on high.
Is this the kind of fast I have chosen,
only a day for people to humble themselves?
Is it only for bowing one's head like a reed
and for lying in sackcloth and ashes?
Is that what you call a fast,
a day acceptable to the Lord?

"Is not this the kind of fasting I have chosen:
to loose the chains of injustice
and untie the cords of the yoke,
to set the oppressed free
and break every yoke?
Is it not to share your food with the hungry
and to provide the poor wanderer with shelter—

when you see the naked, to clothe them,
and not to turn away from your own flesh and blood?
Then your light will break forth like the dawn,
and your healing will quickly appear;
then your righteousness will go before you,
and the glory of the Lord will be your rear guard.
Then you will call, and the Lord will answer;
you will cry for help, and he will say: Here am I."

—Isaiah 58:1–9a

In the earlier passage in Matthew, we see we are not to call attention to ourselves in fasting. In Isaiah we are reminded that acting in accordance to God's will is more important than acting out a ritual such as fasting. When we put the focus back on God as the center of a spiritual discipline, the fast can be implemented in many more ways than just the traditional refusal of food for a time. The period of Lent, which is the time before Easter Sunday, can be used to give up something. We can give up eating meat or eating chocolate or watching television. These are all extensions of the fast and a reflection of sacrifice. When we remember the sacrifice, we are to remember who is at the center of the sacrifice.

I can contemplate the joys of a power failure. When the power went out in my house, the television and the radio fell silent and the Game-Cube stopped! It became dark and the kids were now looking for something to fill the void. Funny how we conceptualize a "void" without our electronics—when, in reality, TV and radio created the void. Over time, electronic media slowly sucked up the time from other activities so we could sit motionless and let our minds be filled with whatever is offered over the airwaves. Our shared value, our culture, is very often shaped and misshaped by what we take in with various forms of media. We are given "facts" by the press so that we can become more discerning consumers or voters. If our time is so completely filled with getting the facts and being entertained, there is little time to discern or contextualize the facts. Electronic devices are so engaging that inadvertently we give our time over to the media. The time given to the media starts as the thin edge of the wedge. It slowly, inexorably, takes more energy and more time from our lives until it inadvertently becomes the center of our lives. What is the first thing you do when you come home? Is it to turn on the radio or TV? Without power, the bondage to the electronic media was broken and our time was returned, which we then spent with reading, studying, reflecting and in other activities. The fast, in its many forms, allows us to sharpen our thoughts and reflect on God.

So we can refuse food and we can refuse the time consumed in other activities to spend it in reading, reflecting, and preparing for our roles in the cosmic play as soldiers for our King.

5. REFLECT

IN THE RECENT PAST, OUR WESTERN CHRISTIAN SUBCULTURE HAS GIVEN meditation a bad name. Too often it is considered a pure emptying of your mind. In reality, biblical meditation is focusing our minds and then filling our minds with God's word. Rather than emptying your minds and having nothing left, a biblical perspective would be to fill your mind with God's message.

Earlier I noted how electronic media started as the thin edge of the wedge to fill our minds. As you focus and reflect on God's message in your life, your mind will be renewed and transformed to understand God's will for you in your current context. The issue is not making time for meditation. Those of us in a fast-paced western culture might excuse ourselves and say that mediation will work for other people and other cultures; however, it is not an issue of time or culture. Most North Americans spend time in meditation, even if they do not realize it; we reflect on getting ahead, on making a dollar, on automobiles, homes, celebrities, or sports.

As a spiritual tool, meditation is more than a form of relaxation. As holy warriors, we use it to transform our minds by fixing our minds on the eternal, transcending truths of God. The truth of transcendence is that it cuts through the problems of the here and now. Our focus changes from petty issues and day-to-day struggles to a bigger picture and a reminder of our purpose in life and what we are ultimately called to do. Meditation allows us to release our problems to God and to reflect on our role in His play, rather than being concerned with the faults of the other actors or the props on the stage.

Rather than contemplating how to get ahead or how to get back at someone, your focus should be to fill your mind with Scripture and contemplate God's word and His faithfulness to all generations. Then your mind will be transformed. Beyond a basic transformation in your thought life, an amazing thing will start to happen. When you are confronted with a situation, your mind will start to reflect back to biblical parallels. When you encounter a difficult situation, you will start to reflect on what happened to Job, Joseph, David, or Daniel. When you encounter a specific temptation, your mind will start to recall the appropriate Scripture for the situation.

Paul wrote in his letter to the Colossians about the practical implications of following Christ.

> *Since, then, you have been raised with Christ,* set your hearts on things above, *where Christ is seated at the right hand of God.* Set your minds on things above, not on earthly things. *For you died, and your life is now hidden with Christ in God. When Christ, who is your life, appears, then you also will appear with him in glory.*
>
> *Put to death, therefore, whatever belongs to your earthly nature: sexual immorality, impurity, lust, evil, desires and greed, which is idolatry. Because of these, the wrath of God is coming. You used to walk in these ways, in the life you once lived. But now you must rid yourselves of all such things as these: anger, rage, malice, slander, and filthy language from your lips. Do not lie to each other,* since you have taken off your old self with its practices and have put on the new self, which is being renewed in knowledge in the image of its Creator.
>
> —Colossians 3:1–10 (emphasis added)

Part of the meditation process is memorization—internalizing the Word that it might be available when needed and for meditation. Psalm 119:9–11 asks, how can a young man become pure? The answer: *"By living according to your word...I have hidden your word in my heart that I might not sin against you."* The psalmist has memorized Scripture that he might have it available.

Another result of reflection is journaling. The immediate discipline of journaling is to record what you find during your reflections on Scripture. The long-term benefit is that, as you review your journal, you can see your progress and refresh your memory of discoveries in Scripture.

I have so far used meditation and reflection almost interchangeably; however, there is a difference. Reflection is one aspect of meditation.

The *meditatio Scipturarum* is considered by all masters as the normal foundation for the interior life. Whereas the study of Scripture centers on exegesis, the meditation of Scripture centers on internalizing and personalizing the passage. The written Word becomes a living word addressed to you.[4]

To know what God would have us do, we need to reflect on and internalize what He has written for us. In the Psalms there are word pictures of meditation. In Psalm 1, the person who meditates on God's Word is like the tree planted by streams of water. He is firmly rooted in the soil and will not blow away. When we meditate on God's Word, it fills our mind and it prepares us to come to Him in prayer. Meditative and reflective prayer expands on a relationship and not on building a shopping list. Another aspect of this discipline is to memorize Scripture that we can reflect on it and meditate on it.

Paul writes in Romans 12:2:

Do not conform any longer to the pattern of this world, but be transformed by the renewing of your mind. Then you will be able to test and approve what God's will is—his good, pleasing and perfect will.

Reading Scripture, refusing other influences, and reflecting on God's word prepares you for that daily Jihad in your mind for the supremacy of your life and your will. As your mind is renewed, the mental strongholds are demolished and you are strengthened with a biblical mindset that has prepared you for daily spiritual battle. The three weapons of reading, refusing, and then reflecting have equipped you to request appropriately the strength and tools needed for both the private and public battles on the daily stage of life.

4   Foster, Richard J. *Celebration of Discipline: The Path to Spiritual Growth.* HarperCollins Publishers, 2009.

6. REQUEST

Absolutely unmixed attention is prayer.[5]

—Simone Weil

PRAYER IS NOT LISTED AS A SPECIFIC WEAPON OR ITEM OF ARMOR LIKE THE Word of God. Some may see it as one of our weapons in battle, while others may see it as the front line of battle. Just as there are many aspects in describing conversation and dialogue, there are many aspects to prayer. So what is prayer? While I have listed prayer under the heading of "request," it is more than that. Prayer is also a two-way conversation and part of being open and honest with God. The personal disciplines are not about rules. They are a reflection of our relationship with an almighty, all-knowing, ever-present and active creator God in our lives. Prayer is not for self-made or self-reliant people. When we make a request, we acknowledge that someone else is in control to grant us our request. How we approach prayer is a reflection of how we understand God.

There is also the challenge of understanding the many facets of prayer. There is a sense in public prayer of ritual and in private prayer of relationship. Mateen Elass in his book, *Understanding the Koran*, gives us a good background to one aspect of the Islamic understanding of prayer:

> ...the story goes that Muhammad was taken by a flying steed at Gabriel's side up to and through the first seven levels of heaven, at each point meeting some of the great prophets of history. At the highest level, Allah is said to have spoken to Muhammad directly, without the mediation of any angel. Here, the prophet received instructions concerning the divine requirements for the prayers of the faithful—all Muslims were to perform the rituals of prayer fifty times a day. Moses

---

5   Weil, Simone. *Gravity and Grace*, p. 117. Trans. Emma Crawford & Mario von der Ruhr. Introduction and postscript by Gustave Thibon. Routledge Classics.

(residing in the sixth level of heaven) inquired of Muhammad what Allah had commanded him, and after being told convinced Muhammad that the burden would be far too great for the people. He urged Muhammad to return to Allah and bargain on behalf of his people, which he did. After five bargaining sessions, the prayer requirement was reduced from fifty to five. Moses still thought this too many, but Muhammad said he was too ashamed to ask any further reductions, and so the number of mandatory prayers for the faithful stands at five.[6]

About 600 years before Muhammad bargained with God on behalf of his people, the apostle Paul did not strike such a good bargain; however, he was more concerned that we spend more time with God so that by association we could become more like Him. Paul's final words to his associates in his first letter to the Thessalonians (5:16–18) were: *"Be joyful always; pray continually; give thanks in all circumstances, for this is God's will for you in Christ Jesus"* (emphasis added). Prayer is both an action and an attitude. Paul's writing moves us from the act to the attitude. So now we can focus on the personal fight, how it reflects on our public fight and witness and the one weapon we can use. In Ephesians 6, Paul lists the full armor of God. After that he writes:

And pray in the Spirit on all occasions with all kinds of prayers and requests. With this in mind, be alert and always keep on praying for all the saints.

—Ephesians 6:18

We could try to cover many attributes of prayer; however, as much as we can try to describe prayer, ultimately it has to be experienced. In the same way we could describe many attributes of water, in its various states; however, nothing can replace the refreshing experience of drinking a cool glass of water on a hot summer's day.

---

6   Elass, Mateen. *Understanding the Koran*, p. 31. Zondervan.

And when you pray, do not be like the hypocrites, for they love to pray standing in the synagogues and on the street corners to be seen by men. I tell you the truth, they have received their reward in full. But when you pray, go into your room, close the door and pray to your Father, who is unseen. Then your Father, who sees what is done in secret, will reward you.

—Matthew 6:5–6

In this case, Jesus focuses us on the relational aspect of prayer. At the time, attention was on the pious and how they prayed. Their public performances increased their social esteem, but they were not prepared for battle. When we are in relational conflict, we can pray. To fight the cosmic battle, we need to pray. Rather than standing on the corner of a public stage, this battle is one-on-one wrestling in our room.

In Genesis 32, Jacob prepared to meet his brother Esau, whom he had not seen for more than fourteen years. The last time he had seen him, Jacob had left in a hurry after swindling the birthright and his father's blessing from his brother. Jacob sent ahead messengers that came back to tell him that Esau was coming with four hundred men. The first thing Jacob did was plot and scheme—then he prayed! *"Save me, I pray, from the hand of my brother Esau, for I am afraid he will come and attack me, and also the mothers with their children"* (Genesis 32:11). Jacob selected and sent a gift ahead to his brother and then he sent his family and possessions ahead of him. Then he remained alone. Yet he was not alone; he had "struggled" or wrestled with men before, but this time he was in a Jihad with God. Many times in prayer we wrestle, struggle, or wring our hands over an issue. In this case, Jacob wrestled with the angel. It says the "man" could not overpower him, but at any instant he could have crippled Jacob. As dawn came, one touch on Jacob's hip changed the struggle, the perspective, and Jacob's name. Now all of Israel struggles with God and will overcome. Jacob wrestled and would not let go until he got his blessing from God, and the blessing was reflected in his name and his gait.

Many may view prayer as special words or an incantation—if you use the formula or follow these four steps, then you will be successful in your prayer. Following magic formulas to get the hidden power of God is not prayer, it is witchcraft or sorcery. Prayer, as a request, is generally seen as changing the circumstances in favor of ourselves or someone else. Intercessory prayer is when we pray on behalf of others. We can either pray for a person's health, wealth, or understanding. Prayer works on us as well as our circumstances. So we can pray to be healed or for some other circumstance to change. However, in prayer, we may ultimately find that our understanding of the circumstance will change and then realize that the catastrophic event in our lives was meant to change us in ways we did not contemplate or anticipate.

One of the questions we encounter in life is "How does God answer prayer?" Some answers are obvious. We can pray that God will provide food for dinner and someone shows up at the door, unprompted, with a prepared meal or invites you out. They might say, "I was thinking about you and thought you might need this or enjoy this." In other cases we may pray for a new car or a new home and it becomes clear that God will not grant it to us despite all of our effort, our circumstances, or our "luck." It becomes very clear that regardless of requests and effort, the answer is "no." Or you might pray and think to grow rich; however, God may not grant you the material wealth you desire, because it would actually get in the way of preparing you to be the warrior and servant for the most high King. How many times have we wished for more money? We can cloak the request in something spiritual and say ""Just think of all the things I could do for God if..."

I don't want to appear fatalistic or irresponsible and discourage you from taking some initiative; however, there are cases when, try as we might, with all the human effort possible and all the prayer expended on our behalf, God will not grant us our request or change a particular circumstance. In fact, it would be a sin to turn our focus from God or try to use God to put more stuff at the center of our attention. In other cases the answer is "no answer." It can lead to that dark night of the soul where we wonder if God is there, if He hears our cries, or if He cares. This third type of answer is even more difficult than a plain "no." Yet in the time of no answer, God may make a priority of healing our hurts, rather than curing our ills. The healing touch of God is meant to make us a whole people before Him, rather than turning us into wealthy paupers who turn aside from Him. Effective prayer is dialogue that draws us nearer to God. As we see God as father, it is reasonable for Jesus to say in Luke 11:9–13:

> So I say to you: Ask and it will be given to you; seek and you will find; knock and the door will be opened to you. For everyone who asks receives; those who seek find; and to those who knock, the door will be opened. Which of you fathers, if your son asks for a fish, will give him a snake instead? Or if he asks for an egg, will give him a scorpion? If you then, though you are evil, know how to give good gifts to your children, how much more will your father in heaven give the Holy Spirit to those who ask him!

It would be fair to say that if God is our father, we can approach Him faithfully and with trust, sometimes even when we don't feel anything. We approach God as a creature to its creator, as a child to the parent. There is no single way to pray—the conversation is based on a relationship, not on rules. While there are rules in any relationship, the essence of the relationship is that we will be committed with our whole being to understand more of our creator and to become more like Him. So naturally a good part of any dialogue would be silence as we listen and wait for a reply. Wouldn't it be reasonable to have the same expectation in our prayer life?

As I reflect on the answers to prayer, I also remember some Old Testament stories on prayer. The first that comes to mind is the book of Job. Job was prosperous and had every reason to pray and thank God for all good things in life until disaster came his way. He lost all his possessions and his sons and daughters. Finally he also lost his health. His wife's solution was for him to *"Curse God and die!"* (Job 2:9). Job cursed the day of his birth, but he did not curse God. Job could appeal to God, but there was no answer. Three of his friends came by to comfort him and then spent their time accusing him of some hidden sin that must have led to this calamity. In all this, Job declared his innocence before his friends and God. Finally, a young man who had waited through the various monologues offered his wisdom. Based on the current wisdom and

Job's circumstances, life did not make sense. Bad things don't happen to good people. We expect—or do we demand?—that God answers prayer. Finally, God does answer and Job is restored.

A second story relates to the prophet Habakkuk. The opening of his book starts with a lament: *"How long, Lord, must I call for help, but you do not listen?"* (Habakkuk 1:2) Habakkuk reviews the current state of injustice and cries to God. Finally God does answer; however, it is not the answer Habakkuk wants to hear. God will use the Babylonians to come in and clean up the town and the nation. It was unthinkable to the prophet that a holy God would use wicked enemies to clean up what was left of this nation that was supposed to be set apart. God replies with a series of "woes" to those who are unjust. Finally in the third chapter, Habakkuk gives a prayer. The result is that Habakkuk understands and accepts God's methods. He praises God and reflects that regardless of his circumstance he will rejoice in God.

We have established that prayer is a discussion or a dialogue with God. It is also a request. In our dialogue we can reflect our praise for who He is, we can come with a complaint and vent our anger at what has been done, we can confess what we have done, we can thank God for what He has done for others and for us, and finally we can ask God for our needs. As mentioned earlier, the basis of asking is based on our relationship with God. Popular religion tells us that God is within and that we have to find the key within. Prayer consists of actions and words. We hear words and we speak words. The heresy has always been the idea that if we do certain things, we can become like God. The corruption of both ancient and modern spirituality is that if we say our prayers in a certain way we are guaranteed success—say the magic words and the doors will be opened to our desires and our will. If you have the special knowledge, you will be like God. Isn't that what Satan promised Eve in the Garden? If you eat of the fruit of the tree you will be like God (Genesis 3:5, paraphrased). Our request is not of ourselves; prayer is a request of God. We may ask for wisdom or insight or the fulfillment of physical needs, and the expectation is that God will grant the request and more.

Paul writes a prayer in his letter to the Ephesians:

*And I pray that you, being rooted and established in love, may have pow-
er, along with all the saints, to grasp how wide and long and high and
deep is the love of Christ, and to know this love that surpasses knowledge—that you may be filled to the measure of all the fullness of God.*

*Now to him who is able to do immeasurably more than all we ask
or imagine, according to his power that is at work within us, to him be
glory in the church and in Christ Jesus throughout all generations, for
ever and ever! Amen.*

—Ephesians 3:17b–21

The prayer is not that we would be God, but that we would be filled
with the Love of Christ and the expectation that God will grant our requests even more than we could ask or imagine. This is beyond the power
of positive thinking. This is beyond us. When we are filled with the love
and the mind of Jesus, we know what He would have us ask from Him.
In asking in the name of Jesus, for His glory, it will be granted. The question now is, with all the troubles we are faced with today, how can we be
effective disciples? How can God use us to glorify Him?

When we are tempted in a breach of personal holiness—we can
pray for strength. When we are in conflict, in a breach of relationship—
we can pray for healing. In the event we are not experiencing life to the
fullest and with more than we could ever ask or imagine—we can think
of Paul, under house arrest, as he writes to the Philippians:

*Do not be anxious about anything, but in everything, by prayer and pe-
tition, with thanksgiving, present your requests to God. And the peace
of God, which transcends all understanding, will guard your hearts and
your minds in Christ Jesus.*

—Philippians 4:6–7

Some people would have us learn various formulas and methods
of prayer that would guarantee results. The result of following Jesus
is that our minds are transformed from the inside out. We are no longer conformed to this world. We have another worldview—an eternal

worldview that allows us to be used by God. To fight the personal, relational, and cosmic battle—we need to pray.

Finally I would like us to pray for four things:

1. **Personal holiness** – To demolish the personal strongholds
   in our lives.
2. **Personal relationships** – With family, friends, and colleagues, that they may be encouraged.
3. **The Church** – For the past actions of the Church as an
   institution where there needs to be restitution and healing
   in relationships.
4. **Our mission** – Whomever we come into contact with,
   that we may be a reflection of God in the world.

7. FAITH

WE CAN GO THROUGH ALL OF THE MOTIONS AND DO ALL OF THE RIGHT THINGS and yet not have faith. As we are actors in the cosmic play, we look at the spiritual disciplines as part of the script. A true actor will absorb the script and cannot help but be changed by it. There is something transformational in the spiritual disciplines. To carry out spiritual disciplines without faith and without a sense of grace would lead to a dead form of legalism.

Faith is not about rules, ritual, and religion, in the traditional sense; faith is a reflection of our relationships. If there are valid criticisms of faith and religion, they relate to experiences with a dead form of function and legalism, or the quick ticket to our eternal reward by strapping on a bomb pack and killing a bunch of innocent people while we make our statement.

An understanding of how we fit into the greater cosmos and the grace bestowed on us should lead to a sense of awe. It is our relationship to the cosmos. There would be a sense that there is nothing we can do that would make us equal to God. Any of our earned righteousness could never equate to the righteousness and holiness of God. We can be set apart, we can read, meditate, fast, and pray, yet none of it will make us worthy of or equal to God. Conversely, the quick ticket to eternity by killing those we think we know are unworthy of God doesn't make us any better a candidate. Our righteousness, as hard as we may try, would be like dirty rags compared to the cleanliness of God. For all the work we do, some may get a little closer to that holy standard, but none of us has arrived. True righteousness is given to us by grace, not by our good deeds; our faith in the graciousness of God and His provision for us allows us to have a relationship with a personal God. Working our way up to heaven will never get us to the top floor. What is needed is faith that God has provided the way to an eternal relationship to Him by His choice. Grace and His graciousness mean that God has chosen us, or allowed us, to have a relationship with Him. It is not that our greatness makes it a privilege for God to be friends with us.

Faith grows through trials and perseverance. There are many stories starting in Genesis that illustrate faith. Noah's life was considered exemplary—he was righteous among the people of the day. When he was told to build a giant life raft (more like a giant basket), he had two options. He could ignore it, or he could build the ark despite concrete evidence at the time that there was no need for such a structure. Noah gave evidence of his personal faith in God through the very public act of building and supplying the Ark. Surely his neighbors questioned Noah's actions, but Noah and his sons persevered through the work of building the Ark and the accompanying trials. The act of building the Ark did not save Noah by itself. During that construction period there was no indication of any impending doom. Building the Ark was a reflection of his faith in the unseen God that saved Noah and his family.

Paul writes in his letters that we are saved by grace through faith. Not on our own works, lest anyone should boast of his deeds. We can reflect on someone of great faith. It is generally not the faith that we see directly—it is the outcome of faith. So what is faith? The writer of the letter to the Hebrews states in Hebrews 11:1–2, *"Now faith is confidence in what we hope for and assurance about what we do not see. This is what the ancients were commended for."* The rest of the chapter enumerates the ancient people of faith. Their faith was not in themselves. So much encouragement today is to have the wrong kind of faith. Our society expects us to have faith that things will work out and to have faith in yourself to achieve your goals.

At issue is not whether we are a people of faith. We all have faith in something. The crux of the issue is where we place it. Is our faith in this material world, in roles and rituals, or is it in the almighty God, the Supreme Being, who created the universe and all therein? So we return to our view of who God is. If we place our faith in the children's Sunday school god, a Sunday morning god there to make us feel good once a week, then our faith will crumble when we are refined by the fires of life. Life is tough. Part of that difficulty is our own doing, some of it is the work of others, and even more difficulties are a result of the structures and systems we are currently living under. If we do not have a faith in God who cuts through all of that stuff and lifts us out of the pit of day-to-day existence, our life will seem worthless. A living relationship with God, the great "I Am," transcends all of our daily misery and will turn our sadness into joy, knowing that the great almighty God, the creator of the Heavens and the Earth, cares about people—collectively and as individuals.

A modern parable of faith reflects on an impending flood. It had been raining for twenty days. With the spring melt and the continual torrential downpour, the lakes were full and rivers were flowing beyond capacity. In a small town, the notice to make way for the flood was given and the townsfolk were asked to evacuate. While most left their homes for higher and safer ground there were, as in any town, a few who chose to remain. The rivers were swollen and took out bridges and spilled over their banks to flood the town. What was left were hundreds of rooftops. A few of the rooftops had one or two occupants on them. As the waters swirled by the rooftops, those few occupants could see the trees and debris rushing past. They watched in horror as someone was swept away. While they may have been safe on their rooftops, they knew they could not rescue anyone.

For a short time the rain let up, and over the sound of the rushing of the waters they could hear the drone of an outboard motor. As they looked up they could hear and then see a small boat coming towards them. The lone occupant brought the boat up to one house and asked the man on the roof to jump in. He replied, "No thank you, it's okay, I am safe up here. Everything is under control and I don't see that there is any problem." The driver of the boat then approached the occupant of the next rooftop. She replied, "This is a rescue boat? I don't think so! I was expecting something a little larger and more stable. Getting in a little boat like this does not fit my idea of a rescue. I would rather wait for a helicopter to come by and pick me up." The boat left that rooftop and went on to the next. At the next house, the pilot of the boat did not need to extend an invitation. As the boat approached the waterline of the roof, its inhabitant started to climb down to enter the small lifeboat.

The day went on and as the pewter grey sky started to get darker the rain returned with a vengeance. The waters rose and became faster.

The roofs collapsed and the buildings crumpled. There was no helicopter and the remaining rooftop occupants met the same fate as the buildings. There was no safe place left in the town as it was washed away from its foundations. It was folly to build a town on floodplain, even if there was expected to be only one devastating flood every one hundred years. It was even greater folly for those remaining not to recognize that they needed to be rescued or to pass up the rescue offered. Yet it is not much different from how we run our lives today. Some of us are enjoying our experience in life and do not see any need for rescue. Others see the need, yet they have not accepted the simplicity of the plan God has provided. Finally, others recognize their need and God's provision and have acted in faith by climbing in the lifeboat that they may have a relationship with God that stretches from now to eternity.

Two out of three people recognized the problem, but only one acted in faith to claim the rescue. The end of this would be best capped with the start of Psalms. Here we see the example of a man who read, reflected and prayed and developed deep roots in a relationship with God. Despite the wind blowing, he was rooted in God and stood the test of the winds of time.

Blessed is the one who does not walk in step with the wicked or stand in the way that sinners take or sit in the company of mockers, but whose delight is in the law of the Lord, and who meditates on his law day and night. That person is like a tree planted by streams of water, which yields its fruit in season and whose leaf does not wither—whatever they do prospers.

Not so the wicked! They are like chaff that the wind blows away.

Therefore the wicked will not stand in the judgment, nor sinners in the assembly of the righteous.

For the Lord watches over the way of the righteous, but the way of the wicked leads to destruction.

—Psalm 1:1–6

Section II:

THE PUBLIC BATTLE & CHRISTOLOGY

"The days are coming," declares the Lord, "when I will make a new covenant with the people of Israel and with the people of Judah. It will not be like the covenant I made with their ancestors when I took them by the hand to lead them out of Egypt, because they broke my covenant, though I was a husband to them," declares the Lord.

"This is the covenant I will make with the people of Israel after that time," declares the Lord. "I will put my law in their minds and write it on their hearts. I will be their God, and they will be my people. No longer will they teach their neighbor, or say to one another, 'Know the Lord,' because they will all know me, from the least of them to the greatest," declares the Lord.

"For I will forgive their wickedness and will remember their sins no more."

—Jeremiah 31:31–34

In your relationships with one another, have the same mindset as Christ Jesus:

Who, being in very nature God, did not consider equality with God something to be used to his own advantage; rather, he made himself nothing, by taking the very nature of a servant, being made in human likeness.

And being found in appearance as a man, he humbled himself by becoming obedient to death—even death on a cross!

Therefore God exalted him to the highest place and gave him the name that is above every name, that at the name of Jesus every knee should bow, in heaven and under the earth, and every tongue acknowledge that Jesus Christ is Lord, to the Glory of God the Father.

—Philippians 2:5–11

VIGNETTE TWO

HEINZ WOKE UP TO ANOTHER TERRIBLE DAY IN THE HOSPITAL. HE HAD ALWAYS hated the idea of hospitals and doctor's appointments. Visiting friends and family in the hospital in the past had not been one of his top priorities. Perhaps a visit to the hospital reminded him of the frailty of life and the human condition. Now at eighty years of age, he was diagnosed with cancer and not expected to last much longer. It was discovered late, and now it was just a matter of time until he would meet the ultimate end.

Heinz was a successful businessman. He had come to this country over fifty years ago with nothing more than a suitcase and ten dollars in his pocket. He worked hard and got a job, then a car. He got married, bought a home, started his business. Then he and his wife had their children, two sons and a daughter. The early years of life in the new country were full of promise. Heinz had faith. With lots of hard work you would eventually be rewarded. His reward was a growing business with eventual financial freedom. He was able to move to a better home, then a bigger home. His company bought a boat. He was able to buy a family vacation place where he, his children, and grandchildren could come and vacation and build memories. That now seemed like a memory in the distant past.

This morning, like the last, would be spent alone with nothing! The orderly came in and served him breakfast. Breakfast—you call this breakfast? A plate with warmed-over food he couldn't recognize. Breakfast in the past was bacon, eggs, hash browns, and toast with coffee, orange juice, and fresh fruit served on fine china and a linen tablecloth either in his room or in the dining room of a fine hotel. Here he was fortunate to have a private room and telephone. His work, his home, and his wealth had bought him many friends. Now, with a tinge of regret, there were no friends, but he would take care of that. He would make sure they wouldn't get anything. Forgiveness was not a word in Heinz's vocabulary. Unfortunately Heinz, like the pharaohs, would realize too late that you can't take it with you.

His wife was too sick to leave home on her own and come visit him. His first son had been disowned from the family ten years ago. There would be no chance he would see him and Heinz had already cut him out of his will. His second son had been buried just last year and his daughter was now too busy with the business and her personal life. Besides, she could not bear to see him like this. The once strong, proud, successful businessman reduced to a fraction of the man he used to be. She wanted to remember him the way he was.

So he prepared himself for another day of being bored and alone with little to do and no one to talk to. He could pick up the phone and make a call; however, most people were away or busy carrying on with their lives. Over time they had arranged their lives and affairs without him. Heinz had worked hard and lived by the motto that he who ends up with the most toys wins. Now he had to face the end of his life and the realization that he still did not have all the toys. He was about to leave the world as he came into it—alone.

Heinz was so busy acting the part of a pharaoh building his empire he forgot, until now, that he was not the sun god. It was now he realized his part in the cosmic play. Up until now, life had not been a struggle because he was too busy working. He now considered if there was any chance for redemption, if he could let go of his stage props, when he thought he heard a knock at the door to his room. Was this the end of his scene of the cosmic play?

★ ★ ★

Ravi knocked lightly on the door to the hospital room and waited for a response. He knocked again lightly, so as not to disturb the occupant but let him know someone was there. Ravi strained to hear the invitation to enter. He heard the reply and came through to see Mohammed, a successful businessman who was held in high regard in his community; however, he was not feeling very well. Three months earlier, Mohammed had started going to his doctor with a chronic complaint. There was nothing the doctor could do but run a number of tests and then give the diagnosis for intestinal cancer. Mohammed would have to go to the hospital for further diagnostics and radical treatment. They had to catch the cancer before it continued to spread. Mohammed had the means to go to the best of hospitals in Singapore. He was checked in on Monday. Tuesday morning the diagnosis was confirmed with surgery scheduled for Friday. Then there would be the months of treatments to follow.

It was now Wednesday and Ravi had made the trip to visit Moham-mad. He prayed for Mohammad in the name of Jesus Christ. At the end of the visit, Ravi had a vision that Mohammad would be back to the mosque for Friday prayers. Ravi shared that vision with Mohammed, yet Moham-med scoffed. The next day, Mohammed felt better. The staff at the hos-pital ran another set of diagnostics and he was cleared. Mohammad was discharged on Thursday night and sure enough, he was back in time for Friday prayers in the local mosque. After that time, Mohammad and the community had gained a new respect for Ravi. Mohammed and others who knew what had happened within the Islamic community of faith had a respect for Christians. Not that they would convert to Christianity; however, there was a healthy respect for the true followers of the book.

★ ★ ★

Edith had been in the hospital for two years now. She was hospitalized after her last fall, when she had again broken some bones. She was not allowed back to her apartment, as there was too great a risk she would fall again and create even greater injury. In these last two years she was slow-ly, inexorably losing her capabilities. Now she shared a hospital room with someone else, with a few photos on the wall, flowers on a shelf, her Bible, and a notebook. The rest of her personal effects from her apart-ment had been collected in boxes and stored away.

Every Monday her grandson would visit. The first visits were discussions marked by her constant request to go home. "I want to go home." She did not mean her apartment. It was in Edith's mind that it was time to go *home*. In God's time she had to remain. After a short time and a prayer, her grandson would return to his home and his family.

As the weeks went by, Edith made no further requests. Now the visit was a time for her grandson to help feed his grandmother. The tables had turned. Forty years ago, Edith would make lunch and feed her two-year-old grandson. Thirty-five years ago, Edith would take her grandson for a walk to the park or along the beach. Now the time for a walk was gone. The time for heart-to-heart talks was here. Time to share memories and hopes of a better place. Time for Edith to share her concerns for her children, grandchildren, and great-grandchildren. Edith had meddled in the affairs of her grandchildren. She had used what means she had to share her faith with her family. Had she done everything right? No. Was there a capacity for her to forgive her family for mistakes and misunderstandings? Definitely. You would hear her desire that it end now and wonder, what was the point of continuing?

One visit in March brought her grandson and his family to see Edith. Her speech had so deteriorated that it was difficult to make out what she said. On this occasion, her great-grandchild Amy recited Psalm 23:

The Lord is my Shepherd, I shall not want.
He makes me lie down in green pastures,
he leads me beside quiet waters,
he restores my soul.
He guides me in paths of righteousness for his name's sake.
Even though I walk through the valley of the shadow of death
I will fear no evil for you are with me;
your rod and staff, they comfort me.
You prepare a table before me in the presence of my enemies.
You anoint my head with oil; my cup overflows.
Surely goodness and love will follow me all the days of my life,
and I will dwell in the house of the Lord forever.

After Amy had finished reciting the Psalm, you could hear Edith work hard to say, "Good." The children all excitedly exclaimed, "Grandma said 'good.'" I am sure she did. She wanted nothing else but to go home—home to her good shepherd. Two weeks later, her breathing became shallower, and the pace quickened as she raced toward her final destination. Friday morning was the end of the final act of her play on this stage as she returned home.

During the memorial, we found out she still felt a sense of purpose for the last days of her life. She left very little in the way of things as a legacy for her family. Her mission was not to collect the most toys. What few things she had were left in a few boxes in a garage. Her desire for her family was found in her notebook by her Bible. Her son found what looked to be a prayer list. She had pages with the names of her children, grandchildren, and great-grandchildren written down. In the last two years of life, she could do no more, and no less, than pray every day that her Lord would take her home and that someday all of her family members would join her. Every day was a battle to live on the front lines of prayer. Most of the family had dismissed Edith as not all there, for she had started to lose her capacity to speak. However, she had not lost her capacity to comprehend what was going on. She invested the last of her energy in making an eternal investment for her family through prayer.

For a moment we had a glimpse of the play from the seat of the King.

8. THE PUBLIC BATTLE

WITH A CLEARER UNDERSTANDING OF GOD, WE CAN GAIN A BETTER understanding of ourselves.

One of the biggest enemies in the understanding of ourselves is materialism. In the western world, life can be so good and things may be going so well that we get addicted to busyness and stuff and life on this planet without realizing it. Our minds can become so distracted with the here and now. In other words, we can get so caught up within the cosmic play with the props that we forget our role, the purpose and the final outcome of the play. The material reality is, it is all going to end and we will be left with nothing. Someday we will leave nothing other than our bones or ashes.

Materialism comes in two forms. One is the pursuit of "stuff" which is what we typically attack.

In a simpler time, advertising merely called attention to the product and extolled its advantages. Now it manufactures a product of its own: the consumer, perpetually unsatisfied, restless, anxious and bored. Advertising serves not so much to advertise products as to promote consumption as a way of life. It "educates" the masses into an unappeasable appetite not only for goods but for new experiences and personal fulfillment. It upholds consumption as the answer to the age-old discontents of loneliness, sickness, weariness, lack of sexual satisfaction; at the same time it creates new forms of discontent peculiar to the modern age. It plays seductively on the malaise of industrial civilization. Is your job boring and meaningless? Does it leave you with feelings of futility and fatigue? Is your life empty? Consumption promises to fill the aching void; hence the attempt to surround commodities with an aura of romance;

with allusions to exotic places and vivid experiences; and with images of female breasts from which all blessings flow.[7]

There are a few stories about how to catch a monkey either in India or Africa. They follow the theme of using either fruit in a hollowed-out coconut or filbert nuts placed in a jar. The bait is placed inside the container and the opening is just large enough for the monkey to put their hand in to grab the treasure. Now, the jar or the coconut is tied down so that as the monkey pulls its hand out with the prize, it can't get its hand out. The hand is now a ball of a fist grabbing tightly to the treasure, and the monkey, even seeing the impending danger, will not release its hand. At this point it is easy for the person who set the trap to put a net over the monkey and sell it or serve it. A lesson learned somewhere in life for us is not to hang onto the stuff so tightly!

The second, more insidious form of materialism is found in our reliance on our rational and scientific method. In the western mindset of empirical rational thought, everything has to be repeatable and measurable. Blaise Pascal, a French mathematician, worked out the possibilities and outcomes of whether to believe in God. From the rational perspective, he determined a grid with four outcomes. God either exists or He does not. Either Pascal believes in God or he does not. Not being able to determine the probability of which statement about God was true, he could review the possible consequences. If he believed in God, and God existed, the final outcome was good. If he did not believe in God, and God existed, the final outcome as he understood it would be to burn in hell! If God did not exist, it didn't matter. So Blaise Pascal, in the true rational mindset of the time, determined that he should believe in God since not believing had the possibility of being to his serious disadvantage. If I cannot set the hypothesis and conduct a repeatable experiment to disprove the hypothesis, then I cannot deduce my thesis. If I can't put God in a box and contain Him, then there can't be a God. By definition God cannot be put in box. The life and claims of Jesus Christ are not repeatable; hence, from a modern rational mindset, the miracles can't be

---

7   Lasch, Christopher. *The Culture of Narcissism: American Life in an Age of Diminishing Expectations.* WW Norton, 1991.

true. The whole course of history is not repeatable; they did not have
CNN around two thousand years ago to record the events, and modern
man cannot trust his predecessors to determine what is truly miraculous.
So we are left with meager rational proofs and outcomes to determine
whether we believe God exists.

Not only is there currently much mistrust for scriptural or ancient
historical accounts, there is a dose of unhealthy skepticism for current
events. Hollywood has become so good at fabricating stories and evidence that it is hard to separate reality from fantasy on the big screen or
what comes through on the internet and television. The first time I saw
the plane crash into the first World Trade Center tower, it looked like
something out of a Hollywood movie. It was too surreal to be true. My
kids showed it to me on television first thing in the morning, but it took
a second input of information before I understood what was happening.
If we see even something contemporary and don't believe it at first, how
are we going to take on faith the accounts of a tax collector, fisherman,
doctor, and rabbi from two thousand years ago?

The issue with materialism, within the theme of this story, is that
we can get so caught up in the props and the backstage technology that
we forget they are only props for our role in the larger cosmic play. The
best example of anti-establishment and anti-materialism is the life of Jesus Christ.

God became a person in Jesus Christ. He did this for two reasons.
First, Jesus was an example of how God intended for us to live. The second and more important reason was that He chose to suffer our consequences since we did not live as God had intended for us to live.

In Philippians 2, Paul encourages us to follow the example of Jesus:

*Who, being in very nature God, did not consider equality with God
something to be used to his own advantage;*

*rather, he made himself nothing by taking on the very nature of a
servant, being made in human likeness.*

*And being found in appearance as a human being, he humbled
himself by becoming obedient to death—even death on a cross!*

—Philippians 2:6–8

Because of the attitude Jesus Christ exemplified, we are to reflect those values in dealing with others. Our faith in God goes beyond a personal "God and me" relationship. Our faith is reflected in our actions and our other relationships.

The issue with the public disciplines is that we can too often focus on externals. We spend our energy on what we say and what we do. In fact, those public disciplines are to be one more reflection of our faith. While our reading of Scripture, meditation, prayer, and fasting are personal and potentially private disciples, those around us cannot help but notice our select times of solitude, giving, and service. The public disciplines start with seeking God and coming into and then reflecting His presence. Our understanding of God as creator sets the standard and expectation of holiness, and also sets the standard of grace and forgiveness. A true transformation is reflected in the public disciplines as we are changed from the inside out. They are a reflection of our faith, not a substitute—a result of our relationship with God and not a set a rules or rituals to gain His favor. In Paul's letter to the Romans, he highlights the struggle and the public outcome:

> *I do not understand what I do. For what I want to do I do not do, but what I hate I do. And if I do what I do not want to do, I agree that the law is good. As it is, it is no longer I myself who do it, but it is sin living in me. For I know that good itself does not dwell in me, that is, in my sinful nature. For I have the desire to do what is good, but I cannot carry it out. For I do not do the good I want to do, but the evil I do not want to do—this I keep on doing. Now if I do what I do not want to do, it is no longer I who do it, but it is sin living in me that does it.*
>
> *So I find this law at work: Although I want to do good, evil is right there with me. For in my inner being I delight in God's law; but I see another law at work in me, waging war against the law of my mind and making me a prisoner of the law of sin at work within me. What a wretched man I am! Who will rescue me from this body that is subject to death? Thanks be to God, who delivers me through Jesus Christ our Lord!*
>
> —Romans 7:15–25

So the Jihad continues, from the warring within our very selves to the public outcome of our actions. Paul wrote about that private battle, and stated that he can have victory through Jesus Christ. The public outcome can be reflected in eight disciplines. Despite the struggle and difficulty, we can have contentment—not that we become content with ourselves.

> *Thomas said to him, "Lord, we don't know where you are going, so how can we know the way?"*
>
> *Jesus answered, "I am the way and the truth and the life. No one comes to the Father except through me. If you really know me, you will know my Father as well. From now on, you do know him and have seen him."*
>
> *Philip said, "Lord, show us the Father and that will be enough for us."*
>
> *Jesus answered: "Don't you know me, Philip, even after I have been among you such a long time? Anyone who has seen me has seen the Father. How can you say, 'Show us the Father'? Don't you believe that I am in the Father, and that the Father is in me? The words I say to you I do not speak on my own authority. Rather, it is the Father, living in me, who is doing his work. Believe me when I say that I am in the Father and the Father is in me; or at least believe on the evidence of the works themselves. Very truly I tell you, whoever believes in me will do the works I have been doing, and they will do even greater things than these, because I am going to the Father. And I will do whatever you ask in my name, so that the Father may be glorified in the Son. You may ask me for anything in my name, and I will do it.*
>
> —John 14:5–14

Just before this passage, Jesus had told the disciples about His betrayal and impending death. After Jesus told them the news, there were many questions from the disciples. Here we have a glimpse of the dialogue between Jesus and His disciples. The reaction from the disciples was one of concern and trouble. Where was Jesus going? Jesus now assures the disciples that each of them, whether they promise to die for him or not, will be able to follow Him to where he is going.

Their relationship started with Jesus here on earth; however, it does not end there—it continues into eternity, in a place Jesus has prepared for them and for us. Even though the future looked bleak—with Jesus leaving—He told them to trust in God and to trust also in Him.

They had a relationship with Him now; the promise was a relationship with Him forever.

9. CHRISTOLOGY

CHRISTOLOGY, A BRANCH OF THEOLOGY, IS A PHILOSOPHY AND STUDY OF THE nature of Jesus Christ.

There are two competing yet complementary claims about the nature of Jesus Christ. The philosophical side of Christology tries to reconcile the truth between Jesus as God and Jesus as man. In particular, we wrestle with how the divine and human are related in His person. This is the great dividing line between Christianity, Islam, and Judaism. Islam will allow that Jesus is a great prophet, with a special status as he is expected to return. Judaism allows that the carpenter turned rabbi had certain things to teach; however, there is no acknowledgement that Jesus was the Messiah they expected. Christology is generally less concerned with the details of Jesus' life than it is with how the human and the divine coexist in one person.

Also of interest is the purpose of Jesus' life. Did He come as the Messiah to deliver the Jews from the Romans? If that was the expectation, He failed. He died a criminal's death on the cross. This is a fact that both Judaism and Christianity accept. Islam would counter that Jesus, as a great prophet, could not have died on the cross. God would not let such a tragedy occur!

Who is Jesus and what was His purpose in life? The short answer would be that He came to lead by example. His conduct on this planet was meant as an example of how we can live godly lives. He set the gold standard for living. The second purpose for His life was to be the sacrificial lamb. Since we have all failed the gold standard, He came to pay the price for our failure.

> Once when Jesus was praying in private and his disciples were with him, he asked them, "Who do the crowds say I am?"
>
> They replied, "Some say John the Baptist; others say Elijah; and still others, that one of the prophets of long ago has come back to life."

"But what about you?" he asked. "Who do you say I am?"
Peter answered, "God's Messiah."

Jesus strictly warned them not to tell this to anyone. And he said,
"The Son of Man must suffer many things and be rejected by the elders,
the chief priests and the teachers of the law, and he must be killed and on
the third day be raised to life."

—Luke 9:18–22

The question of who Jesus is has existed from His incarnation to the present. Paul wrote the following in his letter to the Colossians to set the record straight:

The Son is the image of the invisible God, the firstborn over all creation.
For in him all things were created: things in heaven and on earth, vis-
ible and invisible, whether thrones or powers or rulers or authorities;
all things have been created through him and for him. He is before all
things, and in him all things hold together.

—Colossians 1:15–17

Jesus Christ's nature reflected his unity with God and was reflected in the public disciplines. In the same way, we seek to study and reflect the public disciplines in our lives. We could go through the motions of the next chapters, but the public disciplines will only be truly effective if they are built on the relational faith and transformation of the inner disciplines.

The earlier quotations from Scripture declared that Jesus was God in human form. He came in a Jewish context. From that context, he reviewed and refreshed the meaning of the Scripture given to the Jewish people and the rest of the world.

In Matthew 5, we have the Sermon on the Mount. There is debate as to whether it was delivered at one time or whether it was a summation of His teachings. What's clear is that it was a fresh teaching for the time. The Gospels were written in Greek, but we would expect that the Sermon was actually delivered in Aramaic or Hebrew. If we read it as Hebrew poetry, we get four distinct teachings in the Hebrew parallel form. We are given the image of the Rabbi, one greater than Moses, delivering a new law. The Ten Commandments are not enlarged with a myriad of details; they are expanded in spirit and breadth with nine blessings. The blessings are not the material blessings His audience would expect; they are the natural fulfillment of the longings of those who hunger and seek after God and His will.

> *Do not think that I have come to abolish the Law or the Prophets; I have not come to abolish them but to fulfill them. For truly I tell you, until heaven and earth disappear, not the smallest letter, not the least stroke of a pen, will by any means disappear from the Law until everything is accomplished. Therefore anyone who sets aside one of the least of these commands and teaches others accordingly will be called least in the kingdom of heaven, but whoever practices and teaches these commands will be called great in the kingdom of heaven. For I tell you that unless your righteousness surpasses that of the Pharisees and the teachers of the law, you will certainly not enter the kingdom of heaven.*
> —Matthew 5:17–20

This is a new "law" that doesn't abrogate the old law. It is not a set of rules to be followed to the letter, or a set of rules that can be verified by our public actions. It is more a series of principles, ideals, and motives for our conduct. It is the law that is written on our hearts. Jesus' parables and direct teaching outline values based on a new kingdom ethic that exceeds the thousands of rules and regulations promulgated and enforced by the then-current religious establishment.

In the good news as retold by John in chapter 14, this is about three years into the public ministry of Jesus. Phillip said, *"Lord, show us the Father and that will be enough for us"* (John 14:8). Phillip wants more. He wants an experience like Moses, who could meet God and not die. Phillip needs to see God with his physical eyes. His request shows that even though the disciples had spent these years with Jesus, they still didn't get it. Because Jesus lives in perpetual union of purpose with God the Father, His word and actions are God's words and actions. Jesus reminded the disciples of the miracles. Jesus healed the sick. He fed four thousand. On another occasion, He fed five thousand. He raised Lazarus from the dead. These actions were signs that He indeed was the Son of God, and the things He did were to glorify God the Father. Jesus reminded them in verses 12 to 14 that because of what He had done, and because they had faith in Jesus, they could do even greater things than Jesus had demonstrated. If we have faith in Him, we are called to follow Him in what he does. We are to walk as Jesus walked. We are to do as Jesus calls us. While we are called to have faith and to believe, we are also called to have an active faith. That active faith will be demonstrated in the public disciplines. As Paul writes, *"I can do all this through him who gives me strength"* (Philippians 4:13).

Jesus said, *"Do not store up for yourselves treasures on earth, where moths and vermin destroy, and where thieves break in and steal. But store up for yourselves treasures in heaven..."* (Matthew 6:19–21). Jesus also said, *"What good is it for someone to gain the whole world, yet forfeit their soul?"* (Mark 8:36) Some of us are stuck, and feel trapped, by materialism. It is not that materialism has a grip on us. Rather it is that we are holding so tight to the props of the play—like the monkey holding onto the bait. When dealing with a toddler who has a firm grip on something, the best way to make them let go is to offer something else of greater interest. So it would be pointless to say, "Don't do this" or "Don't do that." It would be better to focus and become engaged in the private and public disciplines. Let them fill your mind and time, and then you can slowly release the grip on the stage props.

The following four pairs of public disciplines are offered to help us let go of the things that have us so firmly trapped.

10. STUDY & SCRIPTURE

You study the Scriptures diligently because you think that in them you have eternal life. These are the very Scriptures that testify about me...
—John 5:39

SOMETIMES WE GET CONFUSED ABOUT THE PURPOSE OF A BIBLE STUDY. ONE thought on Bible study is to get all the right answers so we can pass the heavenly entrance exam. We think the object of the study is Scripture, when we are reminded by Jesus in John 5:39 that the Scripture is the means to know God and His will for us. The purpose of Scripture is to reach our greatest God-given potential and obtain wisdom. If that is the case for Scripture, a Bible study does not necessarily have to be just the study of the Bible. This seems like a violation of the Reformation principle of Sola Scriptura. Sola Scriptura has been taken too far in a literal sense, where you read the Bible and apply your own interpretation to words regardless of the structural or historical context. Sola Scriptura was in reaction to the Catholic Church tradition at the time, when the teaching was traditional and allegorical and may have lacked a solid biblical foundation. The interpretation of Scripture was twisted to fit an interpretation.

The purpose of study is to become a top recruit for the kingdom. I would like to preserve the thrust of Sola Scriptura; however, we can enhance our understanding of Scripture through other tools. Scripture is meant to shape our theology so that our theology is biblical, historical, systematic, and practical.

There are many tools available to help us understand Scripture so that we may have a complete, or at least a better, understanding of what God is communicating to us through His Word. The biblical hermeneutic is that Scripture is plain to understand; however, getting a better understanding of the biblical setting and the dynamic equivalent can be assisted with other study tools. The first point in our study is that it remains biblical. Sola Scriptura was meant to keep us on the right track so we do not diverge off on tangents. When studying a passage of Scripture and coming to an understanding, it is best to test our understanding with the rest of Scripture. My faith and theology, in a public and community context, will be shaped by how we understand all of Scripture. It becomes challenging when we read in the Old Testament about the prophet Samuel killing Agag, the king of the Amalekites, in 1 Samuel 15:32–33. Does that give license for other prophets or priests to kill someone in the name of God? My current understanding of all of Scripture, and in my current context, would say no. In that particular case, Samuel was finishing the task that had been assigned to King Saul. Saul was not obedient to God and had not completed his job in the holy war, so Samuel did it for him.

Let us start by keeping it scriptural. When studying the Bible, we typically use a modern translation. We do not have to be Greek or Hebrew scholars, but that helps! For most of us, a good commentary or two, a Bible dictionary, and a concordance will give us the background to the original text and language and how the passage was translated. There are issues of interpretation that confront the translator, and a good commentary will give you the background to those issues. Without that background, you may take a plain reading of a passage out of context. A good New Testament commentary may also give some Old Testament background. In this case, a passage in the New Testament may quote or allude to the Old Testament. Having that understanding of the Old Testament passage, and its context, will give greater clarity to the Scripture. When you're reading the Gospels and what Jesus said or did, a greater understanding of the context highlights just how radical some of His parables and actions were.

The commentary should also provide the Scripture's historical context. Scripture does give historical landmarks and context, but a commentary may help by giving us background to the events outside of the specific passage. This can be helpful when reading the prophets and the historical passages in the Old Testament of the background of the Assyrian and Babylonian Empires. The Assyrians were in expansionist mode, and they were hated by Israel. An understanding of the split in the kingdom, along with the fall and deportation of Israel and the exile of the ten lost tribes gives some background to the history of the Samaritans. When

Jesus told the parable of the Good Samaritan, he used a person from a nationality of half-breeds that were despised by the pure-bred Israelites as the prime example. He depicted the religious elite in the negative position of those who ignored the needs of the person who was attacked by the bandits. While there is good practical teaching in the parable, its thrust or truly radical nature is better understood in the historical and cultural context of the time.

The first two sets of tools for scriptural and historical context should help you to get through the first two points in your biblical hermeneutic: what does it say, and what did it mean at the time it was written? The systematic study and categorization of Scripture is our theology—it is a system of our making and organization that can draw the biblical, historical, and practical stuff all together. It reflects how we learn and assimilate information. When we are confronted with a biblical truth that becomes apparent in the literal and historical meaning that challenges our theology, we have a decision to make. Do we throw out, discount, or amend our understanding of the passage, or do we wrestle with and amend our systematic framework? We need a system to retain the information. We need to ensure our systematic theology is robust enough to handle the information thrown at it.

An example of a narrow theology that did not serve its users well was that of the rabbis at the time of Jesus. They knew and understood the Scripture both to the letter (they memorized it as children) and in its historical context. This was a time when Greek philosophy would have influenced their theology and given it more reflection and vigor. The Pharisees knew Scripture, but did not accept Jesus as the Christ. Jesus as Messiah did not fit the preconceived notions of those leaders of the day. The lesson for us is that we can get so hung up in stylistic analysis in terms of structural or genre changes that we forget the message of the word of God.

The last aspect of study is to make it practical. Sometimes I feel like I have to grind through a passage. Even when there is rich historical content, I may find it difficult to apply to my current context. Sometimes I need to get through the passage, which may give me my historical context, so I can further understand the next passage which has a more current or practical application. Jesus warned His hearers about the religious leaders of the day. He declared "Woe to the Pharisees" and their concern for the study of law, where they would strain at gnats yet swallow a camel whole. It can be found in context in the Gospel of Matthew 23:23–24. (Again, this is another hyperbole of the time and not to be taken literally.) It would have to apply to me. We need to ensure that our study is practical and not just stuffing our head with facts. The Pharisees had nailed down all the details, yet broke the greater part of the law. They were plotting to murder Jesus. They looked at ways to rationalize the scheme by attempting to trip him up in theological arguments. When it came time to have Jesus executed by the Romans, the charge was not one of heresy but of sedition or treason. The detailed understanding of the traditions and Scripture did not have a deep impact on the daily lives of the religious elite of the day.

In James' letter, he exhorts the Church to be quick to listen and slow to speak. The active study of Scripture is meant to be life-changing and liberating.

> *Anyone who listens to the word but does not do what it says is like someone who looks at his face in a mirror and, after looking at himself, goes away and immediately forgets what he looks like. But whoever looks intently into the perfect law that gives freedom, and continues in it—not forgetting what they have heard, but doing it—they will be blessed in what they do.*
>
> —James 1:23–25

A private and public study of Scripture helps us to sharpen our understanding and application of the words set before us. The public discipline of study allows us to challenge our understanding of the language and the culture of the world at the time and helps us map it to a contemporary structure so that we, as individuals and as a group, can rightly apply the truths of the message in our current context. To borrow a concept from Proverbs 27:17, as *"iron sharpens iron,"* so our study of Scripture together allows us to challenge and to be challenged, so that we may grow in faith and have the wisdom to live a biblical and practical life.

11. Service & Sabbath

It may be amazing for you to see Service and Sabbath listed as complementary disciplines. Most legalists would view Sabbath rest as diametrically opposed to any active service. The Pharisees were so rigid that they were prepared to take Jesus to task when he was going to heal the man with the withered hand.

> *Another time Jesus went into the synagogue, and a man with a shriveled hand was there. Some of them were looking for a reason to accuse Jesus, so they watched him closely to see if he would heal him on the Sabbath. Jesus said to the man with the shriveled hand, "Stand up in front of everyone."*
>
> *Then Jesus asked them, "Which is lawful on the Sabbath: to do good or to do evil, to save life or to kill?" But they remained silent.*
>
> *He looked around at them in anger and, deeply distressed at their stubborn hearts, said to the man, "Stretch out your hand." He stretched it out, and his hand was completely restored. Then the Pharisees went out and began to plot with the Herodians how they might kill Jesus.*
>
> —Mark 3:1–6

It begs the question, what is the purpose of the Sabbath? The Sabbath was meant for rest, a day set aside to thank God and worship Him. The biblical imperative for the Sabbath is outlined in Exodus as God commands Moses that the day is to be set aside and no one, Jew or foreigner, is to work. This was one more public action that made the people of God unique, holy, and set apart from their neighbors. What the Pharisees missed was that their very act of the sacrifice on the altar during the Sabbath could be considered a violation of God's law! They were working and killing on the Sabbath. While the priests were not busy killing animals, their oppressive legalist mindset was killing the spirit of an already politically oppressed people. Their plot to eliminate Jesus would not be an activity to be condoned on the Sabbath or any other day. The imperative for the Sabbath is found in Exodus 20:8–11:

> *Remember the Sabbath day by keeping it holy. Six days you shall labor and do all your work, but the seventh day is a sabbath to the Lord your God. On it you shall not do any work, neither you, nor your son or daughter, nor your male or female servant, nor your animals, nor any foreigner residing in your towns. For in six days the Lord made the heavens and the earth, the sea, and all that is in them, but he rested on the seventh day. Therefore the Lord blessed the Sabbath day and made it holy.*

During the time of the Old Testament, hundreds of regulations were built around the original Ten Commandments to define work—what it was, and what it wasn't. The religious establishment had determined how far you could walk in a day. If I followed that rule, I would not be able to enjoy God's creation by walking through the woods for an afternoon. A legalistic interpretation would mean I could not play soccer with my son on the Sabbath because sports was one of the thirty-nine areas of work that were specifically forbidden. In my current understanding, however, I could set aside a day as a Sabbath and part of the celebration, and what makes it special, is that we could play soccer or hockey together. Meanwhile the merchant class stays in their homes and maps out their work and business transactions for the coming week.

> *Hear this, you who trample the needy and do away with the poor of the land, saying,*
> *"When will the New Moon be over that we may sell grain, and the Sabbath be ended that we may market wheat?" —skimping on the measure, boosting the price and cheating with dishonest scales, buying the poor with silver and the needy for a pair of sandals, selling even the sweepings with the wheat.*
>
> —Amos 8:4–6

Amos was called as a prophet to tell the people of Israel that they had perverted justice and the Sabbath. The Gospel of Mark (2:23 to 3:6) shares a narrative of Jesus and the religious establishment. They are wondering whether Jesus is going to break the Sabbath rules by "working" on the Sabbath. Jesus mentions in Mark 2:27 that the Sabbath was made for man—not man for the Sabbath. By having the man stretch out his hand, and then healing the hand, Jesus was doing creative work on a day of rest. Clearly this was a violation of one of the classes of work prohibited on the Sabbath.

On the evening of the last supper, Jesus demonstrated service to an even greater level. He washed the disciples' feet. Culturally, as the master, He did not have to do that. That was supposed to be the job of a slave, who would serve guests as they came into the home. Peter objected to the foot washing and then asked for Jesus to clean all of him. The point of the exercise was not to have clean feet—it demonstrated servanthood. In a time when the ruler is served, and every whim is satisfied, Jesus' example runs counter to the culture then and now. Jesus embodied and personified the true servant. He claimed that the Son of Man came to serve—not to be served.

Do we totally ignore the Sabbath—the day of rest? No, but we should not ruin it with a legalistic or strict religious interpretation. Parallel passages of Luke 6:1–5 and Matthew 12:1–8 address the time when the religious leaders accused Jesus of allowing his disciples to violate the Sabbath. They were going through a grain field on the Sabbath and the disciples picked some of the heads of wheat to eat them. They were harvesting, working, on the official day of rest. Jesus had to remind the religious leaders that other violations of the Sabbath were allowed. The quote, "I desire mercy, not sacrifice" goes back to before the time of Amos. There is a chronic problem of enjoying and reflecting the true nature of Sabbath and service. We can choose to feel blessed in the presence of God and we can also choose to be a blessing to others as we reflect God's love and mercy in our service.

In Deuteronomy 22:1–4, it is mandated not to ignore your neighbor's donkey or ox if it strays or is found in the ditch. Either bring the animal or item back to your neighbor, or keep it for them until they come looking. This sets a higher level of conduct against the backdrop of the culture of the time. It would be easy in our busyness or piousness to ignore the problem.

The Temple, Synagogue, and Sabbath were meant to be holy. Set apart. Different. Those symbols were meant to be witnesses of the Kingdom of God to the world at the time. An even greater example would be the prescribed acts of service mentioned in Deuteronomy, whether performed in Synagogue, on the Sabbath in the marketplace, or during the workweek.

The Son of Man came to serve, not to be served. The Lord is the Lord of the Sabbath, yet He chose to serve.

12. Simplicity & Solitude

How do we make a break from our rational and material world? How do we block the competing messages long enough to sort out the truth? Where and how do we set aside time to contemplate the bigger issues of life? The disciplines of solitude and simplicity are really the public outcomes of the personal discipline of the fast.

How could Handel compose the *Messiah* at such a quick speed? Could it be that he had time to focus on the task at hand? With all the current technology we have to make our lives "easier," it appears that our lives have become more complicated and interrupted. With all our time spent on answering emails, checking our smartphones, checking our voicemail at home, voicemail on our cell and work, and keeping up with our friends on social media and instant messaging, there is little time to respond, read, reflect, or work. With all of this technology to stay connected, we have become entrapped and enslaved to the tyranny of responding to the now. All of this in the name of making our lives easier!

We need to draw a line between technology and lifestyle to make time to do our work as well as set apart the time for solitude and silence. It is in silence that we can listen to the voice of God, and it is in solitude that we can reflect on His word for us. When we carve out that time, we are setting aside holy time. Holy time, like a holy place, is set aside for a particular purpose. Like the fine china brought out for Thanksgiving and Christmas dinner, time needs to be set aside for solitude. It may not be practical or desirable to spend a day or a week in a monastery; however, we can set aside some time to reflect on life even amidst our regular routines. Whether we're cutting the lawn or going for a run, time can be carved inside that activity for solitude. While I am cutting the lawn, it may not be pure silence; however, I do have time to myself to reflect on God's grace and goodness. While I am running, or if you are at the gym, there is time to listen and reflect. Turn off the music and spend time meditating, contemplating, and reflecting on God's word.

Simplicity in lifestyle pays a big bonus in the use of our time. In Luke 10:1–4, Jesus commissions seventy-two disciples to go and preach the gospel that the kingdom of God is near. There is a purpose and urgency in the mission, so life is not to be complicated or burdened down with too much stuff. There is a call not to bring a second pair of sandals. They were not to spend time packing a bag, or the extra energy carrying a bag. They were to go. While on the road they would encounter others on the way. They were not to divert their attention from the task by standing or sitting by and chatting with whomever they met. The command was not to be rude, the command was to stay focused.

In a similar fashion, Paul wrote to his fellow worker Timothy in 2 Timothy 2:4–7. As a soldier, Timothy was not to get involved with civilian affairs. His focus was to please his master.

The call for simplicity is a call not to be entrapped or ensnared in this world's affairs. Timothy was reminded that the task of the soldier, athlete, and farmer was to focus, play by the rules, and work hard. He would then see the results of the harvest. It was not a monetary harvest of a cash crop. This was a harvest of souls for the kingdom.

How do we practice these dual but related disciplines in our culture? If we simplify our lives we have time for what is truly important. Earlier I enumerated a number of technologies used to stay in touch with others, whether colleagues, family, or friends. The time spent keeping in sync with all these contacts is time lost getting in sync with God and ourselves. To start, it may mean turning off the computer and phones for an hour or two on the weekend to carve time out to read and reflect. This would give you a time of solitude. The Gospels illustrate how Jesus called his disciples away from the demands of the crowds. In the same way, he calls us away from the tyranny of the day to day. In our times of travel or reflection, we can then see how the activities and "stuff" we carry actually distract us from our calling and purpose. Paul gave those three examples to Timothy of mindful, purposeful activity. Each person in his profession has goals and knows certain activities will need to be done to achieve those goals; likewise there could be many activities that would detract from those goals.

Why are solitude and simplicity set apart? They are set apart as they are related. We need to simplify our lifestyles so that we can make some time for solitude. They are set apart as a public discipline in that your friends and neighbors will see that you are different. You are not carried away in the constant noise and activity of life. You are neither walking, standing, nor sitting in the company of others; rather, like the tree planted by the river in Psalm 1, you have set apart the time to delight in the law of the Lord and meditate on it. In the process of coming away from the noise, you are like a caterpillar that is no longer happy to munch on stems and leaves; the time will come when you can be transformed into a butterfly. The discipline of simplicity allows you to let go and leave behind the stuff that keeps you held down; you can then break out of the cocoon to spread your wings and fly.

13. Stewardship & Sacrifice

In a religious setting, whenever we talk about stewardship and sacrifice it is not unusual to expect someone to pass the plate or pressure you for a commitment of your time or money. The immediate reaction is to protect your wallet! The whole idea of giving our money away so someone else can enjoy it or squander it runs counter to our individualistic and materialistic mindset.

From a religious perspective, we are taught that giving for the needs of others is mandated. Whether the motive is altruistic or personal, we're expected to reflect our values in giving. What is the basis for passing the plate? In church circles you might encounter a "stewardship committee." This committee has the dubious assignment of encouraging everyone to give. Depending on your background and lifestyle, they may place certain expectations on you as to what you should do for the church or some project.

When we read through Leviticus, we find many types of sacrifices and offerings we can give. The sacrifice for our sins was mandated. If you do the crime, you must pay the time! Instead of us or our children being sacrificed on the altar, a lamb, an ox, a bull, or two birds were given in our place. The sacrifice was for sins we had committed against God as well as for sins of omission or sins we had committed unknowingly. Once a year, there was a celebration on the Day of Atonement. It was a full-day ceremony full of symbolism where the high priest entered the Holy of Holies of the Temple, first on his behalf and then on behalf of all the people, to sacrifice for sins and to witness that the sins had been taken away and now rested on the scapegoat. This was literally a goat that took the fall for everyone. The sin sacrifices, in their various forms, were meant to pay for our crimes. They were mandatory in the same way as we need to pay our traffic fines or face the consequences. The sacrifice was an obligation. The New Testament reality was that Jesus Christ came as a person and took our place as the sacrifice. Also, the same generation that witnessed the sacrifice of Jesus Christ as the Lamb of God witnessed the destruction of the Temple. There is no longer any need to pay for a sin sacrifice since it has been paid once in full for us all.

Beyond the sacrifice for sin, there were many other offerings. These were generally freewill offerings and part of a celebration. The offerings were not meant to be a glum affair! A first-fruits offering was to thank God for the harvest. It would be very much like our thanksgiving feasts. The fellowship offerings were a freewill offering to thank God for being God and for His blessings. The fellowship offering, like the first fruit, was celebratory and was shared between the priests and the family giving the offering.

There were also rules about how to harvest the fields. You were not to take every stalk of wheat. You were purposely to leave some behind for the gleaners. This was a form of welfare where the poor could go into the fields and clean them, and the reward for their work was taking what was left behind. Finally there was the year of Jubilee. This was a celebration and also a provision for the poor. There is speculation whether it was ever followed, or followed seriously; nevertheless, there were a number of provisions for giving in the Old Testament.

Very often in church circles we hear of the concept of the tithe. The tithe is over and above the sacrifice and offerings. The tithe is a tenth of what we possess or earn that is given for the work of the temple or synagogue. The concept started early in the Old Testament. It is not like we can have flocks pass under the staff and commit one tenth to God today; however, it is easy to calculate and give a tenth of our income (Leviticus 27:32–34). Under this formula, it would only take ten families to form a synagogue. It is simple, but it can be legalistic! If all we give or ask for is a tenth, then we are ignoring the rest of Scripture. To be clear, God doesn't need this money—it was for the support of the priests and the religious system.

What is so messed up about our view of giving is that we actually believe we are giving *our* time, or *our* talents, or *our* treasures. In Jesus' Parable of the Talents found in Matthew 25:14–30, the king gave the servants three sets of bags of money (the talents). To one person he gave five bags, another two bags, and another one bag of money. When the king returned from his journey, there was a time of accounting. The first two servants had invested, worked hard, and doubled the king's investment. In both cases they said, "See, we took your money and here is the result." The third person did nothing with what he was given. He stuck the money in the ground—it was not even given to the bankers or money traders to gain even a basic return on investment. His perception was that the king was going to get a return on investment and work that was not his to receive. The third servant incorrectly perceived the talents, the work, and the return to be not the king's but the servant's.

The root of the problem is that most of us actually believe that what we give is ours to give, and not the king's treasures entrusted to us to invest for the kingdom. This is where the concept of stewardship comes in. The steward is a servant or a slave. He is assigned the task to care for the master's household and business affairs. A good steward worked diligently, on behalf of his master, for the care and increase of his household. The fields and assets were not the steward's to begin with, and neither would they belong to him at the end of his service. The most he could hope for was praise from his master for a job well done.

Back in the time of Jesus, giving was also one more way to differentiate yourself from others. If you were seen as more pious by fasting and giving alms, you would be held in higher esteem in society. Naturally, the more you gave, the higher your estimation. It is no different now when people with significant wealth will give significant sums to a charity to have a building or foundation named after them, or a plaque in their honor placed on a wall.

Imagine Jesus, along with others, watching who is giving to the temple treasury. It is a very public affair as wealthy merchants toss their offerings into the collection box. Along comes a widow and places all her monetary value into the treasury. Her two mites, which are nothing compared to the riches so easily given by the wealthy, are of far greater value or worth than all the previous gifts combined. God does not need our money. He desires our hearts. The widow's gift—in a relative sense, not in its absolute value—was worth far more and was a reflection of her gratitude to God. The lesson to be gained from the widow is that the offering was to be a reflection of an attitude of gratitude to our creator and king. The gift was not given out of duty or guilt. The rules did not require the widow to give all that she had.

The religious leaders also had a vested interest in ensuring the people gave to the temple. Their income depended solely on the revenue to the religious system. Of course they would encourage everyone to give. In fact, they got to share in the offerings. It was in their best interests to ensure more money came to the temple than to taxes or daily living. Given the political climate of the day, consider the question posed to Jesus, and his reply:

> *"Tell us then, what is your opinion? Is it right to pay the imperial tax to Caesar or not?"*
>
> ... *"Show me the coin for paying the tax."* They brought him a *denarius and he asked them, "Whose portrait is this? And whose inscription?"*
>
> *"Caesar's,"* they replied.
>
> Then he said to them, *"So give back to Caesar what is Caesar's, and to God what is God's."*
>
> —Matthew 22:17, 19–21

Roman taxes were tribute to the emperor. The Jews at the time were a vanquished people. The New Testament ethic, as expressed by Jesus and expanded by Paul, was that we owe everything to God. Nothing is ours in the first place. Job summed it up when he said:

> *Naked I came from my mother's womb, and naked I will depart.*
>
> *The Lord gave and the Lord has taken away; may the name of the Lord be praised.*
>
> —Job 1:21

Our giving, sacrifice, and stewardship are a reflection of our gratitude to our creator, redeemer, and king. The public disciplines are a reflection of our attitude of service to resources entrusted to us. The attitude of stewardship goes beyond the day-to-day "stuff" we have to handle. It expands to an understanding that the Earth is the Lord's and all therein. Our attitude of stewardship should then reflect our care for all of God's resources. Our public and private service of giving is a reflection of gratitude and should not be motivated out of reward or guilt. As we have an increasing sense of God's provision for us, it would be reflected in an increasing sense of gratitude which would be reflected in our giving. We have been given the time, talent, and treasure, or the wisdom, work, and wealth, to actually do as we please; however, what is pleasing to God is that our attitude and actions reflect our desire to do as He pleases.

Ultimately, God does not want our sacrifice. We can read in Leviticus 1 that the aroma of the barbecue is pleasing to God; however, He would rather have our living sacrifice than our fasting, or dead animals on the altar. He would rather have us act out justice and mercy than determining to the Nth degree exactly how much we are required to give. God doesn't need any of it! The disciplines of sacrifice and our stewardship are for us—not God. In giving of our time and talent, we're focusing our heart on His Kingdom. Where our treasure is, there our heart is also. God wants more than our money—because it is not our money. He wants us—all of us. As actors on the stage in His cosmic play, we are to be fully committed to the role. All the things around us are merely props in the play.

So now we are stuck in this place with our economy and the props of the play. A good explanation of entry-level economics is that it's all about the allocation of scarce resources. God has unlimited resources, as He created all that we see. He doesn't need any money or things. It is not like the creator of the universe needs some cash to run down to the supermarket to buy a jug of milk or build another church building. The religious thinking is, how much of my money do I have to give back to God? The relationship thinking would be, how do I invest the resources God has given me to make greatest long-term returns? So the money given every week to help children out of poverty may have a greater return than any multi-million-dollar investment in a building with my name on it. Regardless of the size or type of gift, Paul reminds us in 2 Corinthians 9:7 that God loves a cheerful giver. The gift is not given out of duty but in sheer delight that we can be part of some greater cause or mission. The gift reflects our ultimate values, and pales in comparison to the ultimate sacrifice and gift of Jesus on the cross to bridge the relationship gap between man and God.

14. FORGIVENESS

WHILE GOD AS CREATOR SETS THE STANDARD AND EXPECTATION OF HOLINESS, He also sets the standard of grace and forgiveness. A very real reflection of our faith is our measure of forgiveness. Regardless of how careful we are, someone will hurt us—either intentionally or unintentionally. How we deal with that hurt will be reflected in our forgiveness of others.

From our perspective, it was a totally irrational act for God to come in human form to provide an example and pay for the crimes of humanity. Jesus' life purpose was to provide the way for total forgiveness and to teach it to His followers. Two parables in the gospels exemplify forgiveness; the first parable that has crept into our culture is that of the prodigal son. The story is also known as the parable of the lost son, but more aptly could be considered the parable of the prodigal father. Prodigal means "lavish." So the prodigal son was one who spent his inheritance lavishly. The older son, and some Christians, tend to focus on that. An alternate understanding of the parable would be how the Father lavishes his love on his sons. This is in the context of the parables of the lost coin and lost sheep. The focus is on the Father. While we can focus on the actions and loose living of the son, the story actually tells us more about the love and the forgiveness of the father. The story foreshadows God's love for us through Jesus Christ. The second story, of the unmerciful servant found in Matthew 18, is in reply to Peter's query to Jesus about how often he should forgive someone. Should it be seven times? The reply was seventy times seven and then the story.

> *Therefore, the kingdom of heaven is like a king who wanted to settle accounts with his servants. As he began the settlement, a man who owed him ten thousand bags of gold was brought to him. Since he was not able to pay, the master ordered that he and his wife and his children and all that he had be sold to repay the debt.*

At this the servant fell on his knees before him. "Be patient with me," he begged, "and I will pay back everything." The servant's master took pity on him, canceled the debt and let him go.

But when that servant went out, he found one of his fellow servants who owed him a hundred silver coins. He grabbed him and began to choke him. "Pay back what you owe me!" he demanded.

His fellow servant fell to his knees and begged him, "Be patient with me, and I will pay it back."

But he refused. Instead, he went off and had the man thrown into prison until he could pay the debt. When the other servants saw what had happened, they were outraged and went and told their master everything that had happened.

Then the master called the servant in. "You wicked servant," he said, "I canceled all that debt of yours because you begged me to. Shouldn't you have had mercy on your fellow servant just as I had on you?"

—Matthew 18:23–33

The point of the parable was not that we should keep score. All of our transgressions start as a transgression against God. At great cost God has forgiven us of all our transgressions. In light of His forgiveness for us, could we not, as small as we are, also forgive those who have hurt us?

I have approached the spirit of forgiveness as a spiritual reflection of our faith; however, from a practical, mental health perspective, we also need to gain a spirit of gratitude and forgiveness. Gratitude is that deep sense of thankfulness for what we have, rather than a spirit of discontent for what we don't. Western marketing is bent on creating a need by generating a spirit of discontent for what we have. We are bombarded with messages of what we should be and what we should own and what we deserve. We are driven by guilt for not attaining the right status or owning the right stuff. To assuage our guilt, we can buy something or blame someone else for our shortcomings. I believe there is a sense of despair for personal failure. The root of that failure is the spirit of discontent. There is also a sense of entitlement for what we want. It generates a spirit of envy and a lack of forgiveness. We learn that we cannot forgive ourselves, much less anyone else. We tend to blame our parents for not giving us what we want or for bringing us into the world.

To cultivate a spirit of forgiveness, we have to start with ourselves. If we accept all the messages of western marketing, then we will grow to be bitter people with a lack of grace and gratitude for what we have. We become malcontents continually striving and desiring something just outside our grasp. If we do not cultivate an attitude of forgiveness, we risk growing in bitterness rather than grace.

Forgiveness in a financial sense means to forgive a debt. Writing off a debt comes at a cost; however, it is better than deluding ourselves that the other person has the understanding, will, or capacity to right the wrong or pay back the debt. So in a social and spiritual sense, writing off the wrongs of those who have hurt us does comes at a cost; however, the cost is ultimately less than any interest earned in harboring the debt.

Jesus Christ is the epitome of grace and forgiveness. During the last supper, Judas was at the seat of honor, even though Jesus knew Judas was going to betray him. Jesus also knew Peter was going to deny he had ever known Jesus three times within the day. Jesus disrobed and took the role of the lowliest servant to wash the stinky feet of his followers, including Judas and Peter. After the foot washing, Jesus asked them if they understood what had occurred.

> You call me "Teacher" and "Lord," and rightly so, for that is what I am. Now that I, your Lord and Teacher, have washed your feet, you should wash one another's feet. I have set you an example that you should do as I have done to you.
>
> —John 13:13–15

The washing of feet was a lowly task and set as an example of service, a reflection of our faith and our love. While some may apply the foot washing ceremony today literally, the wider application is to reflect the love of Christ through service to others. The way we treat others is a public reflection of how we understand the way God, through Jesus Christ, has treated us. We seek to serve others as we have been served. We seek to love others as Christ loves us. We seek to forgive others as we have been forgiven.

Many of us could drown in a spirit of despair for our personal failures. Others could drown in a pool of pride and envy. Pride, envy, and despair are the runoff of the torrential downpour of a basic of lack of forgiveness. In many cases we cannot forgive others; in other cases we cannot forgive ourselves. Jesus knew, as He served the disciples, that they would fail Him and betray Him. Despite His foreknowledge, He had the love and capacity to serve and forgive. Judas tried to force the hand of Jesus to set up the kingdom now by betraying Him to the current ruling class. When Judas came to his senses, he realized what he had done. He could not reverse the course of events and he could not forgive himself. He died in despair.

Peter had also betrayed Jesus by denying him three times, but Peter found forgiveness in Christ. As Jesus was beaten and bloodied and then hung on the cross, He had the capacity to love and forgive. His words are an example to many persecuted Christians through the ages to today.

Father, forgive them, for they do not know what they are doing.
—Luke 23:34

The example and teaching of Jesus ran against the grain of society two thousand years ago, and continues to run against the culture today. To turn the other cheek, to go the second mile, to love and forgive—all run counter to the gospel of prosperity and success. While the prosperity gospel has the visible proof of success in the here and now, it is time to reevaluate whether we should be spending time "succeeding" in a venture that, in the light of eternity, will ultimately fail and turn into dust, rather than taking the risk of failing at something that ultimately will be a success.

Jesus' death on the cross, from a public and a material perspective, was seen as a failure and a disaster. It would be a failure if the story ended on the cross, but the story doesn't end on Friday.

Sunday morning, Christ was vindicated and the victory was in the resurrection. The power of love is shown in the very real and costly act of forgiveness and taking our place as a sacrifice. So what does the life, death, and resurrection of Jesus Christ mean for us in very practical terms?

It can be summed up in Paul's letter to the Ephesians:

Get rid of all bitterness, rage and anger, brawling and slander, along with every form of malice. Be kind and compassionate to one another, forgiving each other, just as in Christ God forgave you. Follow God's example, therefore, as dearly loved children and walk in the way of love, just as Christ loved us and gave himself up for us as a fragrant offering and sacrifice to God.

—Ephesians 4:31–5:2

Section III:

THE CORPORATE BATTLE & PNEUMATOLOGY

And afterward,
I will pour out my Spirit on all people.
Your sons and daughters will prophesy,
Your old men will dream dreams,
Your young men will see visions.
Even on my servants, both men and women,
I will pour out my Spirit in those days.

—Joel 2:28–29

So in Christ Jesus you are all children of God through faith, for all of
you who were baptized into Christ have clothed yourselves with Christ.
There is neither Jew nor Gentile, neither slave nor free, nor is there
male and female, for you are all one in Christ Jesus. If you belong to
Christ, then you are Abraham's seed, and heirs according to the promise.

—Galatians 3:26–29

VIGNETTE THREE

FRANK STARED ABSENTLY AT THE HALF-EMPTY WATER GLASS. AT THE AGE OF forty-five, he was reflecting on the glass and his life. What was the meaning of life? What a stupid thing to think! Perhaps it was the scotch whiskey doing something to him. After all, he had everything he needed, yet his life was like the water glass—half empty.

Somewhere in one of those success seminars he had learned that the glass was not half empty, it was half full. He had learned that he did not look at life from the right perspective. Yet he found materialism and all the pursuit of stuff was bankrupt. So he chased the meaning of life in relationships and spiritual things.

Now he had learned that if he thought the right way and developed successful habits, he too would become successful. For whatever success was, he didn't feel successful. The reality was, regardless of all the positive thinking, his situation in life appeared bleak. He was questioning his purpose in life. He knew the meaning of life went beyond getting more things, but he didn't know what was beyond getting more things. He had tried many relationships. They all ended in disappointment. He had expected more; however, he knew he should have expected less.

He was working his way up Maslow's hierarchy to become a self-actualized individual, but it was looking lonely at the top of the pyramid. Part of his self-actualization was to meditate. Meditate and reflect on life, on himself, on his mantra, and clear his mind of all the material distractions. When he cleared his mind of this material world, he found there was nothing left! Was the ultimate destiny of each person on this planet nothingness? No, he had to be plugged into something; he was just not sure what it was. Like the water glass, Frank had half the solution: he knew something was missing, but he was not sure what it was.

You do your thing at work, go to the pub, hang out, have a beer with the boys, and then head home. He had been doing this for the last twenty-five years and then he realized how time had crept up on him.

There had to be more to life than another twenty years of this stuff! He could do the social chat on the internet. What was the point of that? Being a part of a virtual community offered some sense of belonging based on the pretenses he had to continue to live on the net, but what was the point of being a part of a community that was no more real than his profile? What was this world all about? If it wasn't for the cooling-off period, he would be staring at a pistol on the table beside the water glass.

The half-empty glass that needed to be filled was a reflection of his life. The self-actualization was not enough and the online community was not real. Life appeared pointless and monotonous, and Frank was not having a quality experience; perhaps it was time to end this experience, or maybe it was time to make a mid-course correction. He vaguely remembered a better time when he was a kid. Childhood experiences took on a different meaning after forty years. The terrible monsters in the closet and hiding under the bed didn't seem so big or real anymore, but the haunting feeling of something terrible lurking behind the door was still there. He remembered the safety and comfort at home and in the routine of going to school, playing with friends, and going to church.

Church was a very dim memory now. The last time Frank could remember going to church, it was a very somber and serious affair after a colleague from work had died. What did that ceremony mean, anyways? There was the one day for reflection; after that, life and work continued on as before. Frank didn't remember that any of his colleagues were particularly religious. He wasn't, but what would happen if he died? Would there be a funeral? Would he be buried or burned—not a pleasant thought, being confined in a box and stuck six feet under. What would happen if he wasn't really dead? He just imagined being buried or burned alive! A cell phone wouldn't survive the flames, and he wasn't sure it would have enough power to transmit through a casket and six feet of earth.

Just at that moment, Frank thought he saw that childhood monster peer through the opening in the closet door. There it was—that deep-seated dread. That dread kept pushing down like a lead weight in Frank's stomach. This had become a bad dream that Frank wanted to escape.

* * *

Hussein was a university student who loved to engage in lively debates over Christianity and Islam. If there was any doubt about the veracity of the Quran, all he would have to do was recite a passage in the most lyrical sense. No one could debate the natural beauty of the sound of the word. Nothing could come close to the Quran—this was the miracle of the prophet. When discussing the virtues of the Quran with his western friends, he challenged them that the Bible was corrupt. One of Islam's messages was that the people of Israel had corrupted the original message of God, so Mohammad was called to set the record straight.

The Christians accepted Hussein. They listened and studied the Quran. Their challenge to Hussein was to read the gospels and find the corruption. The translations were clear that Isa in the Quran was the Jesus in the Gospel; however, in the Gospel Jesus was depicted as more than a prophet. He had the seal of authenticity of the miracles. He healed people, fed thousands, his teaching was outstanding. The Injil—the good news—also had some very hard news: four different witness accounts that Jesus died. That was hard to understand. The most difficult part to understand was not the Injil, but the church of Jesus. What does it mean to be part of the community in Islam? Islam is all-encompassing in terms of faith and daily works. It is not the disconnected faith seen in western culture where you see Christians go to church on Sunday and profane God on Monday.

Hussein saw a ring of authenticity in the Injil. Perhaps the Scriptures were not corrupted—they showed the failing of the Jews and Jesus' disciples. If the Injil was corrupted, wouldn't the bad parts be removed? The Injil revealed the miracle of the resurrection and the continuous miracle of restoration and reconciliation through Jesus the Christ. It declared that Jesus was more than a prophet. He was God and He was human. If this was the truth, then the west certainly did not live or believe the truth. The west was living a deception. The people of the book had corrupted the transmission of the Injil. Hussein now had a new Jihad. How could he remain part of the Muslim community and believe there was one greater than the prophet? The people of the book and Islam all agree that Allah is the creator and Allah is supreme, but Jesus showed another aspect of Allah. It would be apostasy to ascribe to Isa, Jesus Christ, a higher position than the prophet. The new battle was not with his Christian colleagues at school. The battle went further and deeper. It was civil war for his heart and soul. It could erupt to a battle within his community. If he put Jesus first, it meant everything else was second. If he chose to follow the Jesus of the Gospel, even if he did not renounce Islam, Islam would renounce him as an apostate. He could not join with his Christian friends, as that would be evidence and they would be convicted for proselytizing. Yet Hussein's heart no longer rejoiced in the recitations and rituals of Islam.

What was Hussein to do? He had a better understanding of community than his western friends. To declare allegiance to Jesus openly would mean being shunned by the community, if not murdered by one of its members. In the private war he could declare Jesus as Lord, yet continue to practice Islam. But then he would be no better than many Christians in the west. They may believe in Jesus, but they did not show it. The challenge for Hussein, now, was how to be a citizen of the Kingdom of God as he had come to understand it, and remain a loyal citizen within his current nation. The real challenge was that his country did not recognize dual citizenship in either the political or spiritual realms. Hussein was now caught in the same struggle as the Christians in the early church.

★ ★ ★

John awoke to peer at the numbers on the alarm clock. 3:45 AM. This was another morning when he woke to a sense of impending doom. There was this dread of the dawn of a new day. Fortunately it would be three hours before he would have to deal with anything. Unfortunately, he was sentenced to the next two or three hours of being awake to reflect on the sense of imprisonment in his current circumstances; however, this morning was different. He did not have to deal with customers or suppliers. Today was officially a day of rest—a day he could join in the community of worship to reflect on God's goodness. He could be mired in the difficulties of making things work and having enough money to pay the bills.

It hadn't always been like this. He had had a good job with good pay. He could pay the bills, give generously, and save for retirement. In his middle years, he had been happy with what he was doing and where he was going; however, a mid-life crisis was created when he was fired from his position. The reasons for his termination were vague if not unclear. What was clear was that he was no longer needed or wanted. He was no longer of any value to the company, nor for that matter his family.

It had been seven years since that time, yet the event was seared into his memory as though with a branding iron. Back then he was basically happy with his life and his script of the cosmic play, yet the director, or someone in the improv group, saw fit to change his role and the direction of the play. John was still trying to get his head around his new role to determine how he could best play the part. The struggle in this role was evident. There were far fewer resources, and his role and the goal was still unclear. This part of the play seemed more like a wild merry-go-round ride; your role was just to hang on! It did not appear scripted in any great detail. There was nothing left to do but grab onto the encouragement and presence of a few friends.

15. The Corporate Battle

SOMETIMES WE ARE FORTUNATE ENOUGH TO HAVE A MID-LIFE CRISIS, RATHER than waiting to the end of our days to determine that our current life is worthless or bankrupt. In a previous set of scenarios, Heinz had come to the realization too late that materialism and the singular pursuit of stuff was bankrupt. Frank was going through a serious mid-life crisis.

Like hamsters on wheel, we can be continually running and running and getting nowhere. The joy of a mid-life crisis is that it is in our mid-life and not at the end, so we can wake up to the reality of what is really important. Mid-career professionals may have spent their lives chasing around to be on top of the heap, then come to realize that when they get there, nothing is left. There is nowhere else to go; they have come to the top of their game. There is just more running on the wheel! When they have gathered all the stuff they think they need, they try to get more because it is there or they go searching for the meaning of life. Since many people associate mainline Christianity with the current materialistic culture, they will start their search for meaning in other places.

In reaction to the realization of the bankruptcy of western rationalism and materialism, society has grown aware of other modern philosophies. A pluralistic philosophy is more accepting of thoughts outside the rational philosophical box. It can be as accepting of the teachings of Jesus, Gandhi, or anyone else. It is now up to you to go through the philosophical and theological buffet, and you can sample a number of things and put them on your plate—all-you-can-eat. Come up as many times as you want to take what you want back to your table. At your table you can try what you have selected and then determine what you like. If you do this entirely on your own, without any previous training or feedback, you could wind up with pickled herring, horseradish, hot dog relish, and strawberry sorbet on your plate. Each item appeals to your taste, but they may not work well together. The challenge becomes finding a philosophical framework of life that fulfills our basic spiritual and community needs, yet appeals to our tastes.

In the recent past, when western thought was influenced by the scientific method, the organized church minimized the mystical experience and spent her energies on a rational and scientific apologetic for the faith. At first when the official church opposed the results of scientific inquiry, it had rejected Galileo Galilei's proofs that the earth was not the center of the universe. Galileo was not the first to propose that the earth was not the center of the universe; however, his telescope allowed others to make observations that gave a rationale for the apparent orbits of the stars and planets. The scientific community went on to seek their own version of the truth at the risk of excommunication. Later, church culture adopted the rational mindset. The Bible has since been studied and rationalized as any other book. We try to explain the miraculous or, if there is no explanation, the miracle is dismissed. God has been studied, reviewed, and put on trial. Man has become the judge, and humanistic rationalism has been appointed prosecutor with God in the prisoner's dock.

The Church is depicted in the Bible as the bride of Christ. The bride is looking forward to the wedding day and keeping herself pure for her groom. The Church, in wanting to be accepted by society, has sullied her bridal gown with the same materialistic mindset and taken the trinkets of materialistic wealth. Western society has tried the rationalist and materialist worldview and now found it wanting, so it has moved on into a postmodern or post-materialist or post-rationalist mindset.

As the Church morphs in reaction to its current surrounding culture, it again risks losing long-term relevance. The Church, as the formal organization, can be expected to change its tune to reflect the desires of our culture. Now it has emerged to "reinvent" itself and wash its gown of the dirt of scientific rationalism that was the basis for dismissing the miracles, and rediscover its mystic and holistic foundations.

Does this sound like a harsh condemnation of the formal church? It should. Before the Church, the embassy of God was the state of Israel. For a nation forged through the fire of the exodus through the Red Sea and the desert, it did not take long to forget God. If the Church is the bride of Christ, there is also an Old Testament parallel. In the book of Hosea,

God directs Hosea the prophet to get married. Getting married was a typical expectation for the time, but to get married to a known promiscuous woman was extremely controversial in Hosea's day. The book starts with a biographical note about the prophet and switches to the nation of Israel. Then it switches back to Hosea buying back his wife. Then it continues to use the parallel of the prophet going to the market to redeem his wife with Israel. While the real life experiences of Hosea are not an exact parallel between God and His chosen people, there is enough of a reality show for the nation to get the point. Unfortunately, the nation of Israel at the time did not get the point.

Two thousand years ago, the truth was made freely available and in turn made people free. The freedom of the teaching of Jesus Christ and His church was that true worship was not based on where or how people worshipped. Jesus taught that true worship was in spirit and in truth. True worshippers were not just Jewish males. Paul wrote that the Church was inclusive and included male and female, Jew and gentile, slave and free. The Church was for all believers of every nationality, culture, and social level.

Jesus taught beyond doing good things. He declared the ultimate reality was that the Kingdom of God was approaching. This picture on earth was a reflection or a model of the ultimate heavenly reality. Lest we get too "pie in the sky," Jesus also taught—and Paul and the apostles reflected in their writings—that being workmen, worshippers, ambassadors, and soldiers for the Kingdom meant we would reflect the culture and values of that kingdom in our current nation states. Part of the message of Jesus was radical and subversive. We are to get inside the current organizations and change them with a reflection of our values. The hope, as holy warriors, is that our values reflect victory through the personal disciplines and that our thoughts and actions have been transformed so we can transform the culture around us in the same way as a dash of salt or seasoning transforms a meal.

For our time on this stage, one of our roles includes being citizens and ambassadors of the kingdom of God more than citizens of any one nation here on earth. As heavenly citizens, we have been imbued with the Holy Spirit of God and have also been given gifts and talents to build up each other and the heavenly kingdom.

16. PNEUMATOLOGY

PNEUMATOLOGY IS NOT A WORD I HEAR IN EVERYDAY CONVERSATION. IT refers to the study of the Holy Spirit. *Pneuma* is Greek for breath, which is non-material. Pneumatology may also be referred to as a doctrine of spirits or spiritual beings. Given our culture's current search for meaning beyond materialism, this subject has taken on more relevance; however, most people would not use the word pneumatology—they would rather say that we have come of age, or that we are in a new age.

It may sound weird to be filled with Holy Spirit of God; however, it is no weirder, and less nebulous, than "the Force be with you" or being aware of the Dark Side. The *Star Wars* version of spiritually leaves a few things unnamed, but the audience all gets that there is a spiritual dimension to the battle.

If there is to be a criticism or an error in the current "new" spirituality, it would be that the new spirituality appears to be all about me. As you attain nirvana, you reach perfection. The western mindset has made it a very personal meditation and reflection and a complete absence of community. Evangelical Christians are no different when they reduce the good news of the gospel to "It's all about Jesus and me." Yet the gospel declaration was that the new kingdom was coming. The kingdom is about community and the community was to be bound in a common bond—knit by God's Holy Spirit that dwells in each citizen. The mark of citizenship is the change in character brought on by God's Holy Spirit. It is not the spirit of fear—it is a deep abiding sense of calm. It is reflected by each individual as they exhibit the fruit of the Holy Spirit transforming them from within.

We can go searching for new and old forms of spirituality; however, to borrow from Ecclesiastes, there is nothing new under the sun. The writer of the book searched for "fulfillment" in gaining understanding, in making monuments, and in parties. He found no lasting fulfillment in any of these activities. In the same way, our culture has placed a high value on rational thought, understanding things, and building our monuments. Yet, as a society, are we any happier? The search for meaning in life goes beyond the here and now. The search goes to find the truth in the relationship or context of ideas. We are moving beyond materialism to gain an understanding of life and meaning. The scientific method can be used to observe and repeat the theories of how life can replicate. It cannot go beyond the first cause.

Answers to the questions of the post-rational or post-material culture are found in context of the work of the Holy Spirit. The work and witness of the Church is found in the unifying spirit of God. In Paul's first letter to the Corinthian church, he covers the topic of the gifts of the Spirit and the Spirit of Love as the unifying force of the Church. The church in Corinth suffered from some "unfriendly fire"—divisions in the church. Paul writes to remind them of their unity in Christ through the Holy Spirit and the work of Christ on the cross on their behalf.

As soldiers and witnesses in the army of God, we do not fight the daily battles alone. As we grow strong our job is not to fight each other. It is not to beat up our enemy. We are called to protect the weak and use the gifts we have been given to build up those around us. How is the Church to accomplish all this? By being filled or imbued with the Holy Spirit.

On a practical level, what does it mean to be imbued with the Holy Spirit? To be filled with the Holy Spirit means that we, both as individuals and as members of communities, are filled and overflowing with the presence of God's Holy Spirit, and that this is reflected in our lives. We could use being "filled" and "imbued" interchangeably; the main difference is that when a vessel is *filled* the nature of the vessel is not changed. It is still a container for the water. There is a barrier between the vessel and the liquid it holds. However, when the vessel or person is *imbued*, the container itself is permeated with the liquid. The container is changed.

The reflection of the filling of our lives with the Holy Spirit is seen in the growth of the fruit of the spirit in our lives and in the gifting of the gifts of the Holy Spirit. It is close to the truth to hear someone say that we all have God within us, but we have to understand what is meant by that. There is a difference between when it means we are all gods, in the sense of the God of Creation, or when it means the Spirit of God can be resident in us. We can invite God into our lives just as much as we could invite another spirit into our lives. You can tell whether someone has invited the Spirit of God into their life. The fruit of the spirit is the evidence of the Holy Spirit in the character of our lives. The fruit, as listed in Galatians 5, is a reflection of the character of God in our lives.

But the fruit of the Spirit is love, joy, peace, forbearance, kindness, goodness, faithfulness, gentleness and self-control. Against such things there is no law.

—Galatians 5:22–23

The reflection of these traits is that the fruit is borne as a result of the Spirit of God being resident in our lives. These traits, the fruit of the spirit, are reflected in all believers. The spiritual gifts, which are also evidence of the Holy Spirit working in our lives, are meant to build up and encourage others in our community. Their purpose is not for our own edification, but to train, help, encourage, or equip others in God's Kingdom.

The difference is that all of the fruit is available to all believers. The spiritual gifts are given as needed. Not everyone has a gift for prophesy, or administration, or service. If each person had all the gifts, we would not need each other! That would be counter to building a community. In a community we grow, and are enriched, as we share the gifts and talents given to us. The Church is meant to be an embassy of the heavenly kingdom. It is meant to reflect the diversity of gifts and culture in the same way. Life in the early church was the reflection of a community that went far beyond meeting in buildings. The identity of the early church was in their sharing. Initially it was sharing the message and some of their possessions in common. Later, the community would be bound together in their sharing of suffering and persecution for their faith. The unity of believers was through their experience and God's Holy Spirit in their lives.

17. WORSHIP

Most discussions of worship tend to revolve around style, content, and liturgy in general. Rather than reviewing one style or liturgy as opposed to the other, the discussion needs to be broadened in the context of our relationships. Worship is a personal, public, and corporate discipline. It is personal in that it starts with us as individuals praising God. It starts with us, as creatures of a creator, being "wee timorous beasties" that tremble in the presence of the almighty God. I am not advocating a worm theology; however, as we near His presence we understand how unclean and unworthy we are. It is best described in the first half of Psalm 8:

> *Lord, our Lord,*
> *How majestic is your name in all of the earth!*
> *You have set your glory in the heavens.*
> *Through the praise of children and infants*
> *You have established a stronghold against your enemies,*
> *To silence the foe and the avenger.*
> *When I consider your heavens,*
> *The work of your fingers,*
> *The moon and the stars,*
> *Which you have set in place,*
> *What are mere mortals that you are mindful of them,*
> *Human beings that you care for them?*
> —Psalm 8:1–4

When we gain that awestruck sense of who we really are in light of how holy God really is, we gain the fear of God and start to fathom how great and wonderful His provision is for us. It is incredible to think that the creator of the entire universe actually cares for, and is involved in, the lives of mere specks on this solitary planet. We can consider the prophet

Isaiah. When he was commissioned by God to speak to his people, Isaiah was awestruck and proclaimed the following:

> *In the year that King Uzziah died, I saw the Lord, high and exalted, seated on a throne; and the train of his robe filled the temple... "Woe to me!" I cried. "I am ruined! For I am a man of unclean lips, and my eyes have seen the King, the Lord Almighty."*
>
> —Isaiah 6:1, 5

Worship is public in that others see our act of worship and the celebration of our gratefulness to God for what He has done for us. Our public practice of worship is a reflection of our relationship with God. Circumstances may be difficult and times may be tough. We would be hypocrites if we were happy about tough circumstances; however, we reflect the joy of being called by name into the presence of God. There is a sense of awareness and celebration. It is our praise for God and what he has done for us that is the corporate and very public spiritual weapon in the cosmic play.

I would like to put worship in the context of a team sport. We need to get out of the stands and onto the field and become active with those around us in the game. It is corporate in that we, as a body of believers, are called and will be called into His presence to give Him all the glory, honor, and praise due to His name. It is the corporate "we" that makes for worship. Often western Christianity concentrates on Jesus and me—a personal response—as opposed to our collective response in community to God. This is the time we share songs, hymns, and words of praise to encourage one another, and share our praise before, and for, the Creator and King.

Preparation for worship starts before one shows up at any place of worship. Psalm 122, one of over a dozen Psalms of ascents which can be used in preparation, opens with *"I rejoiced with those who said to me, 'Let us go to the house of the Lord.'"* At the offer to attend communal worship, the reaction was to rejoice. Worship is a celebration of our being in the presence of God.

Now that Jesus Christ has come as both the High Priest and as the offering, the writer of Hebrews encourages us in our new worship. Hebrews 10:22-25 states:

> *Let us draw near to God with a sincere heart and with the full assurance*
> *that faith brings... And let us consider how we may spur one another on*
> *toward love and good deeds, not giving up meeting together, as some are*
> *in the habit of doing, but encouraging one another—and all the more as*
> *you see the Day approaching.*

Let us consider how we may spur one another to love and good
deeds. In the King James Version, it invites us to "provoke" one another
to love and good deeds. Galatians 5:26 gives the negative: *"Let us not*
become conceited, provoking and envying each other." There is a public compo-
nent of community: that we all come together to encourage one another.
The verb translated as "to spur" one another or "to provoke" one another
is very active. It is not passive, but an aggressive and active function of
the members of the church.

The corporate worship is but a dim reality to what John saw in Revelation 4 and 5.

> *Then I saw a Lamb, looking as if it had been slain, standing at the center*
> *of the throne, encircled by the four living creatures and the elders. The*
> *Lamb had seven horns and seven eyes, which are the seven spirits of God*
> *sent out into all the earth. He went and took the scroll from the right hand*
> *of him who sat on the throne. And when he had taken it, the four living*
> *creatures and the twenty-four elders fell down before the Lamb. Each one*
> *had a harp and they were holding golden bowls full of incense, which are*
> *the prayers of God's people. And they sang a new song, saying:*
> *"You are worthy to take the scroll*
> *And to open its seals,*
> *Because you were slain,*
> *And with your blood you purchased for God*
> *Persons from every tribe and language and people and nation.*
> *You have made them to be a kingdom and priests to serve our God*
> *And they will reign on the earth."*
> *Then I looked and heard the voice of many angels, numbering thou-*
> *sands, and ten thousand times ten thousand. They encircled the throne*
> *and the living creatures and the elders. In a loud voice they were saying:*

"Worthy is the Lamb, who was slain,

To receive power and wealth and wisdom and strength and honor and glory and praise!"

Then I heard every creature in heaven and on earth and under the earth and on the sea, and all that is in them, saying:

"To him who sits on the throne and to the Lamb

Be praise and honor and glory and power, for ever and ever!"

The four living creatures said, "Amen," and the elders fell down and worshiped.

—Revelation 5:6–14

Whatever we call worship is but a poor reflection of that scene. In our modern thinking of worship, we look at what would attract the large crowds. Once we have the audience, we try to scheme on how to motivate them to actively worship. We can rightly be accused of promoting attendance to a worship or celebration service in the same way as a football game. We get a big name speaker or performer to draw the crowds, and pray God's Holy Spirit will be present. We make the event easy to attend with low commitment. You can pick up your coffee and muffin in the lobby on your way in. The audience can sit down, take it easy, have their snack, and engage with the band or speaker on their terms. The event is a success when there is high attendance. It is even a greater success if the audience feels motivated and feels God's Spirit was present during the service. In these cases, as in most, it is deemed that the home team won!

Below is a summary of a quotation from the Scandinavian philosopher and theologian Soren Kierkegaard on worship:

We have it all wrong where we see the congregation as the audience, the people on the platform as the performers, and God (His Holy Spirit) as the prompter, when in fact the worshipers are the performers, the people on the platform are the prompters, and God is the Audience.[8]

---

8   Kierkegaard, Soren. *Purity of Heart*, pp. 180-181. Trans. Douglas V. Steere. Harper & Row, 1956.

I see too often the misconception Kierkegaard relates to. The amazing thing is that Kierkegaard's observation was penned over one hundred years ago! The people on the platform are the performers and unfortunately the glory goes to them, not to God. One of the reformation cries was "Soli Deo Gloria." Only to God be the glory! So often worship degenerates to the level of a football or hockey game, where there are hundreds or thousands of people in the stands who need the spiritual exercise, but they end up watching and cheering on a dozen or so people on the platform who could use some rest.

Worship starts before I even show up for the public event. It starts with rejoicing at the opportunity to join other believers in a community of worship. It starts even before the rejoicing, with an understanding of who God is and how I fit into His picture. Paul concludes a section in Romans with the following praise:

> *Oh, the depth of the riches of the wisdom and knowledge of God!*
> *How unsearchable His judgements, and his paths beyond tracing out!*
> *"Who has known the mind of the Lord?*
> *Or who has been his counselor?*
> *Who has ever given to God,*
> *That God should repay him?"*
> *For from him and through him and to him are all things.*
> *To him be the glory forever! Amen.*
> —Romans 11:33–36

After this word of praise, Paul gives the practical application:

> *Therefore, I urge you, brothers and sisters, in view of God's mercy, to offer your bodies as a living sacrifice, holy and pleasing to God—this is your true and proper worship.*
> —Romans 12:1

In the Old Testament, worship was accompanied with gifts and a living animal sacrifice. The Old Testament sacrificial system was abolished with the supreme sacrifice, once and for all, of Jesus Christ; however, there was instituted a new living sacrifice. It is the daily sacrifice of a warrior's will for his king.

Nowadays the focus on worship is twofold. It is a celebration service and the organizers are bent on making sure that when you walk into church you get a "knock your socks off" experience that isn't anything like Grandma's church or the old stodgy church you remembered as a kid. The good news of worship, in the Old Testament context or as a kid, was that it inspired awe in an awesome, all-powerful creator of the universe. It was reflected in the church building architecture as well as in the worship service. We may remember that the service was formal, and it may have been subdued as was the cultural norm, to show respect for the creator and king. Going to church was a serious matter. The bad news was that the repetition and meaning of the liturgy left the participants feeling as dead as the sacrifices on the ancient altar. People would go through the motions with little understanding or commitment. People were painfully aware that they did not meet up to the standards of the grey-bearded man upstairs. There was a sense that at least showing up and going through the actions might be enough to fulfill one's duty. There was a blind hope that maybe God would be pleased with our worship and that He would grant us an eternal pass into His presence. If the old-fashioned "dead" service was a reflection of the eternal reality, who would want to spend an eternity there?

I am concerned that worship today tries to reflect all the celebration and thankfulness with little reflection on the cost of the sacrifice. We are encouraged to express our joy for what God has done and His provision for us without the sense of awe of God or a sense of the futility of what it would take for us to even consider how to redeem ourselves. The price has been paid by a sacrifice and our debts have been forgiven. That is what we are thankful for; however, with all the noise of celebration, we have little chance to contemplate the size of the debt that has been paid. What may be missing in modern worship is the awe of the enormity of the debt. We cannot pay a debt worth ten billion dollars; neither can we pay our debt by any sacrifice to God. When we encounter face to face how short we are of the standard of a perfect and holy God, I would expect our experience to be like Isaiah when he was brought into the presence of God.

Worship, in whatever form on this planet, will never attain the standards we expect God expects from us. It is like a three-year-old plucking dandelions and flowers from the garden and presenting them as a bouquet to the child's mother. The parent knows it is not a dozen long-stem roses, but it is the best that can be given. The intentions are there. The gift is accepted with the full understanding that this is a reflection of a child's love. It is given in a love relationship and is accepted with grace in the spirit of giving.

Very often we can get engaged in discussions about worship and it will revolve around the subjective matter of the style of the music or the type of prayers. We project our cultural expectations as God's expectations for worship. We discuss the various things people wore and what they said and did. We are getting caught up in the props of the play. In all cases our worship is a dim reality of that worship in the heavenly throne room. Our songs, words, and prayers are like the bouquet of weeds and flowers offered to God. Worship is a public reflection of our love and commitment to Him; it becomes an encouragement to others and it is accepted by God in the spirit of love that we have given the best we can give.

So then, as a community of worship, we are knit together by the common experience and profession of meeting a truly awesome God. We acknowledge that we fall short of the mark set for us. We may even be so brave as to confess that we actively stray away from that mark! Individually and collectively, we are overwhelmed by God's grace in His provision from now throughout all eternity to become adopted members of His family and full citizens of His kingdom. Worship, regardless of the culture, style, or form, is in "spirit and in truth" and should reflect the full and true nature of our collective relationship with God. We can debate the music, the sermon, the prayer, how we pray, how we sing, and whether we dance. Regardless of the debate, we are called to become active participants in worship and realize that whatever we give or do, our worship is but a dim reflection of the ultimate reality of that heavenly worship and our relationship with our creator and king. For a moment, we can contemplate our worship from the seat of the king.

18. WORK

A GREAT PERVERSION IN OUR MODERN TIMES HAS BEEN HOLDING UP THE Protestant work ethic. There is nothing wrong with working and hard work; however, the perversion is that it has been ripped apart from a biblical norm and infused with secular values. Work exists for work's sake or work exists so I can make money to spend on what I want. This thinking is divorced from being God's steward, appointed to tend the garden or care for His sheep.

In my youth I was given the quote from Genesis 3:19: *"By the sweat of your brow you will eat your food."* It was given to me to reinforce the value of hard work—the true work ethic. Even before I understood the full context of the passage, I took it as the curse it really was.

Another trend we can track is the trivialization of work. From the economic perspective, Karl Marx observed the "deskilling" of the workforce and the intensification of capital investment. The work and the worker get parceled into smaller, more meaningless units. In the office environment, work is made trivial as work life takes on a new meaning— the focus is to look powerful or successful, rather than actually executing any skilled work.

Our horizons shorten to the task at hand or may go so far as using work to help extend our social network. We need to expand our horizons on work to include our vocation and calling. It is the combination of our talents aligned with our passions. Either we have been trained and disciplined in our life's calling, or by circumstances we have been thrown into a situation and given the grace and natural gifts to deal with it, and our efforts will yield results for our king. Work is also more than an individual effort. We may be assigned or called to execute certain work-related tasks; however, those tasks are for others within our community. For those of us who work only for a payday, work is a basic exchange of our time and energy for money. Even in that basic exchange there is an interaction within our work community. For those who like their work, gain personal fulfillment from it, and see it as a calling, they can look beyond the specific task and see how their actions impact others they work with and those they serve. Work and worship are both public theatre. We perform our work to serve others. Whether the work is entertainment, service, or a supply of goods, it is done in the context of a community.

Our work is our mission. How we work is a reflection of who we work for. Jesus gave the Parable of the Talents, reflecting a biblical value on work. In fact, our use of the word "talent" comes from this monetary measure of wealth in this parable in Matthew 25. The master went away and entrusted various amounts with each of his servants. They had the complete freedom to do as they pleased with the treasure on behalf of their master. In the case of two of them, they invested what they were given immediately and it produced a full return. They doubled what was given. In the case of the third servant, he chose to stick the money in the ground. He did nothing—he didn't even consider entrusting the money to the current banking establishment. Over the time even the one talent given was devalued. The first two servants were rewarded with praise and more talents. The third servant was rebuked and rejected.

Originally, man (Adam) was placed in the garden, given full authority, and assigned to tend to it. With the work came the responsibilities and rewards of tending the garden. The "work" went beyond a nine-to-five job; "tending the garden" can include raising crops as well as raising children, building houses, and building up our spouse or our business. Our work is a very real and material reflection of our worship as we build one another up within our community. The quality of work then becomes a reflection of ourselves as well the quality of the individual we are working for.

The curse mentioned in Genesis 3 is at the root of the toil and struggle we have in, and with, work. Whether we are struggling with a computer malfunction, a misunderstanding with a client or colleague, or reviewing the damage from a hail storm, our work feels riddled with problems. The circumstances in which we find ourselves are not always ideal; in fact in some cases our work is dependent on solving the problems of other people's misery. In workplace literature, the stress and adversity we encounter is seldom a result of overcoming the big hairy audacious goal. The source of most work stress is dealing with the continuous drizzle of small problems and issues that get in the way of achieving our goals.

The problems stem from poor relationships, a lack of mutual esteem, or a low sense of the value of the specific task or work. This results in misunderstandings and a poor quality of service that may support others in the organization. The support worker who does not feel appreciated forms a low sense of worth for the task and their colleagues. This may result in carelessness in the outcome of the task at hand. Those around are poorly served and get frustrated with the person and then treat them with contempt. The carelessness and contempt can soon spread like a virus so that the toil at work increases, leading to diminishing results. This is an outcome of the curse. It is not just the land that is cursed! Work and life become a brutal existence until we return to the ground which was cursed.

There is a longing to escape the curse of the soil and the toil. One solution is the weekly purchase of a lottery ticket sold as a ticket to paradise and freedom from the curse. The odds of winning big in the lottery are typically greater than ten million to one! There may be hope that you can redeem the winning lottery ticket; however, the odds are better to find personal redemption in being connected and part of a redeemed community. There is hope, here and now, for a taste of the future redemption. Partial redemption may be found in fulfilling work.

Most people would not turn down the opportunity to work for the President of the United States. There would be a sense that you are close to power and that the work within the President's office would make a difference for millions. The chances of working for the President are even worse than winning a lottery; however, we do have a chance to change our focus to work for the most-high king—God almighty. Within the community of faith, the members of the kingdom are called to be servants of God the King. Regardless of our current vocation, we are to do work worthy of Him.

Brother Lawrence was a lay brother in a monastery in France. Most of his time was consumed with the daily toil of the kitchen. He became lord of the pots and pans. Later in life, as his health declined, his work shifted to repairing the sandals of over one hundred monks in the monastery. This was humble and demeaning work, yet it had to get done.

Brother Lawrence was not a learned man. Since he was not trained in Latin, he had been inducted into the monastery as a lay brother. His work was to be at the beck and call of the friars. Yet it was his practice of the presence of God in his work in the kitchen that brought Brother Lawrence to the attention of others within the monastery. His wisdom as reflected in his work was later compiled by Father Joseph de Beaufort and published as *The Practice of the Presence of God*.

In the seventeenth century, Brother Lawrence did not have much time to formally worship God; however, he set an example for others to emulate in the reflection of our work. Our work extends beyond the formal hours in active service. Our work can also extend to time spent volunteering in the community or public service. In all our activity, we are called to reflect that our work would be seasoned with the quality and grace of a master craftsman for our king. On the soccer pitch, I encourage our team that we are delivering a command performance before our King. Our work, and play, is to be an outward and material reflection of our worship.

John 2:1–11 tells the story of Jesus at the wedding at Cana. The story tells about an early miracle. It also reflects the quality of the miracle. The water Jesus transformed was no ordinary wine. It was the best quality wine of the wedding feast. While not everyone understood what happened at the wedding, the disciples and those close to Jesus understood the full meaning of the miracle.

Finally, the definition of work goes beyond the expanded scope of "doing things." Work is within the context of a community. That community starts with where we work and expands throughout a network or building relationships. The quality of our work and our relationships can make us subversive change agents, warriors, and ambassadors for the kingdom. After the people of Israel fled Egypt, they were given the task of building the tabernacle, a portable series of curtains and props. God gave clear instructions to Moses on what was to be done and He gave people the skill to complete the task.

A second example of our work as worship would be in the legacy of Johann Sebastian Bach. Bach was a German composer who lived from 1685 to 1750, and his compositions became the epitome of the Baroque style of music. He worked for both the court and the church. His final appointment included working in Leipzig for the school and church. His work had an impact in the lives of people from that time to now. His last two works included *The Art of Fugue,* which was left unfinished and published after his death. There have been attempts to finish the last movement of this work; however, Bach stopped the work and dictated his final work, which was *Before thy throne I now appear.* At the end of every work, sacred or secular, Bach also added three letters, S.D.G, for "Soli Deo Gloria." He could have taken all the praise for his talent, but his Reformation principles were deeply ingrained in his life and reflected in his work. Glory was reflected where glory was due.

Our work, whether for pay or passion, has been given as a very material way to reflect our worship. God has also given us the skills and desire to execute our work and worship with excellence for His Glory.

19. Witness

The act of coming out of Egypt made Israel a nation, and the spoiling of Egypt was part of that witness. The conquering of the Promised Land was a witness, as well as honoring the pact with the Gibeonites. Israel is still a nation, whether it is in the current political reality or represented as the pockets of Judaism spread throughout the world with every synagogue as an embassy.

Christians (the Church) are a new nation that transcends all national boundaries. The old-fashioned priests were intermediaries between us and God. They were meant to speak God's word and work as advocates on our behalf. With the work of Jesus Christ, we are now all priests and ambassadors for the new heavenly kingdom. We could talk about heaven; however, we are called to live our faith and the new kingdom values here on earth. Jesus declared more than moral teaching. His was a call to the new kingdom.

The church of Jesus Christ, as a community of witnesses, confesses that we are a community of failures! Each of us acknowledges that we have failed morally and that we could not attain God's standard of holiness and perfection. We have all failed. It is not the case that we are innocent. On examination, given the motive and means, we would fail. The righteousness is not of ourselves; the Christian confession is that our righteousness comes from faith in Jesus Christ. It is not a matter of doing good to earn your way to heaven. The act of the witness is not to convince the jury or judge of your innocence in the case. We are not selling memberships to the heavenly club on commission. The act of the witness (*martur*) is to tell what they know. In our case, as citizens of the kingdom, we are to bear witness to what we know about the king and his kingdom.

There is another expectation of God's witness. It is one thing to tell the court what you know, but the expectation is that you would live out what you know. The value of the kingdom can best be reflected in the love of God, and His provision for us, in our lives and relations with others. Our job is to be priests or ambassadors for the kingdom.

One of the great forms of witness is how people deal with adversity. It is through great adversity or great opportunity that our true values are shown. Jesus was responding to a comment of the disciples about the temple and future events when He gave the following teaching:

> *But before all this, they will seize you and persecute you. They will hand you over to synagogues and put you in prison, and you will be brought before kings and governors, and all on account of my name. And so you will bear testimony to me. But make up your mind not to worry beforehand how you will defend yourselves. For I will give you words and wisdom that none of your adversaries will be able to resist or contradict. You will be betrayed even by parents, brothers and sisters, relatives and friends, and they will put some of you to death. Everyone will hate you because of me. But not a hair of your head will perish. Stand firm, and you will win life.*
>
> —Luke 21:12–19

Understanding the historical and grammatical context, this passage didn't literally mean no hair will perish on our head. We shed hair every day. Christians were martyrs in the modern understanding of the word— they died for what they believed. They died knowing they would be alive in Christ in the new kingdom. They had a sense of assurance that by standing firm in their convictions they would make it through to eternity unscathed based on their faith in their Lord Jesus Christ.

One of my concerns for western society is the current preeminence of the value or sanctity of life. Our focus tends to be to survive our current circumstances and threats literally unscathed. When we place the value of life ahead of everything else, our society will become dishonest and corrupt and we will live in turmoil. Our values can then become held hostage.

In 73 AD, some Jewish Zealots that opposed Rome chose death and freedom over life and slavery to the Romans. Their testimony lives on in Massada to this day. During the reign of King Nebuchadnezzar, choices had to be made. Three Hebrew captives made a choice to disobey the

King's command. They could choose life and obey their king, or they could choose truth and fidelity to their God and disobey the king. They valued their understanding of the truth over life. Shadrach, Meshach, and Abednego forsook life for the truth and were saved from the furnace, and their witness lives today.

In these cases, the witnesses were prepared to forfeit their lives to testify for what they knew was true. No one would place their life ahead of a chocolate bar or candy. Our lives are worth more than that! No one would trade their lives for a lie. There is point where we may have to decide if the truth, liberty, and peace are worth more or worth less than our lives. In a legal setting, a witness is sworn to tell the truth regardless of the consequences. In current western society, the cost of telling the truth is not very severe. When we are filled with the Holy Spirit of God, there will be a sense of peace. With that inner peace, no state or terrorist has any control over our life.

During the persecution of the early church, the believers made a choice between worshipping the Roman Emperor as a god, or not sacrificing or paying tribute to the emperor as a witness that there was only one true God. The witness then was not based on a cleverly designed marketing program. It was borne out of deep-seated convictions. What others saw was that the witnesses had or grasped something worth far more than their stuff or their life. The martyrs back then valued the truth, freedom, and peace more than they valued their lives. Their convictions gave them the peace and freedom to trade their current lives and suffer short-term torture based on the assurance of their citizenship in the kingdom to come.

When I was in elementary school, I heard a story of the fisherman and the starfish. A quick Google search gives us a few variants of the same story. Oyster or clam fishermen realized that starfish could destroy their catch, so they harvested the starfish, chopped them up, and disposed of them by throwing them back in the ocean. Little did the fishermen realize at the time that by chopping up the starfish and throwing them back into the ocean, they helped reproduce the starfish. Now they had a bigger problem than before. I think the Roman Empire chopping up Christians created a bigger problem for them than they had before. The

Christians became martyrs for the Kingdom of God. As Rome persecuted the Christians, their numbers grew. For every Christian killed, the tally of martyrs for the cause continued to rise.

Where did they get the strength to be such a witness? Ultimately it came from a sense of the presence of God from within. They were filled with the Holy Spirit and it was reflected in their actions at work and at worship. They were called to work as if working for God Himself. They cared for others within their community as well as for those who were dispossessed outside their immediate community. Their work in caring for the sick, and in rescuing abandoned babies, reflected countercultural values for the day. Their acknowledgement that there was only one true God, the God who created the universe, brought upon themselves the full force of a state that said whoever was in power at the time was a God.

What would nullify the witness? If the witnesses became concerned over other things, they may have lost the motivation to tell the story. The witness could be like the seed that was planted and grew up among the thorns. Eventually the thorns, the cares of this life, choked out the witness. The other thing that could nullify the witness was if there were no cares at all. If life went so well that there was no sense or need for God or others, the witness would become a self-made person. They would be like the fool in the parable of the rich farmer. He decided he would spend his resources building bigger barns. When he was done building the barns and storing up his treasure, it would be time to leave it all to someone else. In Proverbs 30:7–8, the seer requests that God provide for him. Not too little, that he would dishonor God, and not too much that he would forget God.

The corporate discipline of being a witness is the natural result of being a citizen of the heavenly kingdom. We are ambassadors for the kingdom all the time. In the same way our language or accent gives us away when we travel, our motivations and actions give us away as members of a holy nation. The act of the witness is reflected in our work and worship. It is reflected in our choices on the big issues as well as the myriad of everyday details and actions. The little details of caring for others, bearing their burdens, and allowing others to help us, reflect a community in continuous relationship with God and, through His Holy Spirit, reflect the values of the kingdom now and to come.

20. WARFARE

THERE IS A DOCTRINE OF WARFARE AND A JUST WAR. BEFORE WE RETURN TO warfare in the broad sense, we should review the first two battlefronts. The first section of the book dealt with the personal war that goes on in each of our souls. Impure thoughts, hatred, jealousy, and fits of rage all start with us! If that is not tamed, there is no hope for lasting peace between men or nations. The start of Jihad is that struggle within. The second section of the book covered the public stage on which we play. People may not see you read, fast, meditate, or pray, but they will see the outcome of your actions. It is our public actions that fan the flames of public war.

In the ninth Sura of the Quran, titled Repentance, there is encouragement to continue the holy war on behalf of Islam. As the last recital of the Prophet, it is the final word. There are no other Suras to abrogate the selections from this chapter.

Then, when the sacred months are drawn away,
Slay the idolaters wherever you find them,
And take them, and confine them, and lie in wait for them at every place of ambush.
But if they repent, and perform the prayer, and pay the alms, then let them go their way;
God is All-forgiving, All-compassionate.
The number of the months, with God, is twelve in the Book of God, the day that He created the heavens and the earth; four of them are sacred. That is the right religion.
So wrong not each other during them. And fight the unbelievers totally even as they fight you totally; and know that God is with the godfearing.
The month postponed is an increase of unbelief whereby the unbelievers go astray ...

Decked out fair to them are their evil deeds; and God guides not the people of the unbelievers.

O believers, fight the unbelievers who are near to you, and let them find in you a harshness; and know that God is with the godfearing.

Whenever a sura is sent down, they look one at another: "Does anyone see you?"

Then they turn away. God has turned away their hearts, for that they are a people who do not understand.

So if they turn their backs, say: "God is enough for me. There is no god but He. In Him I have put my trust. He is the Lord of the Mighty Throne."

Imagine western troops coming to "help install democracy" in an Islamic country. All it takes is for the local imam to recite the above portion of the Quran and remind his listeners that the unbelievers are coming. It is their duty to fight back with a level of ferocity previously unknown to them.

The apostle John was exiled to Patmos, a small penal island off of the coast of Ephesus. Near the end of his life, he wrote the apocalypse also known as the Revelation of John. It is a special style of literature that would have been familiar to the people of the time. It was meant to give courage to the troops of Christian witnesses. They were dying as a result of their faith, and John wrote to encourage them, give them some history of the battle, and remind them that the battle had been won. Some of the history of holy war is given in this flashback of the battle with the dragon (Satan) and his loss. This is a reminder that the holy war is not just our war. It is not men against evil. It is much broader, and includes angelic forces fighting against the great deceiver.

Then war broke out in heaven. Michael and his angels fought against the dragon, and the dragon and his angels fought back. But he was not strong enough, and they lost their place in heaven. The great dragon was hurled down—that ancient serpent called the devil, or Satan, who

leads the whole world astray. He was hurled to the earth, and his angels
with him.

—Revelation 12:7–9

Revelation gives scenes from the battlefront. Over time there have been many battles of different types, but there are three battles that truly matter. The first battle was won when Christ died on the cross as the ultimate sacrifice for our sins. The second battle, which believers were struggling with at the time Revelation was written, was for the truth, freedom, and peace. During the years of the early church, believers faced the persecutions of Nero and Domitian. Believers died for the truth that the Emperor was not god, and they chose to die so that they could continue to worship God the creator. While the precise context is not the same for us today, we are still embroiled in a struggle for truth and freedom. The third battle is outlined as the final victorious battle in Revelation.

Comparing the last texts of the Quran and the Bible, there is a major difference in understanding and approach to holy war. Holy war is not to be confused with just war. Just war is a doctrine or philosophy that allows regular warfare when certain conditions and conduct are met. War may be permissible for self-defense or to promote peace and justice. There would be terms of conduct of a just war, limits on what could be done in the name of the cause. In the case of just war, the ends do not justify the means. Neither passage speaks of holy war as a just war. The Quran looks forward to a peace when the entire world submits to God. That submission is in a very real material sense of the here and now. Eight months out of the year, holy war can be brutal. Revelation gives a glimpse of the final battle with angels and demons. It is meant to give hope to Christians now who have to deal with the daily battle.

At a high level, there are different types of warfare. There are political battles, just war, and holy war. As ambassadors for the kingdom of God, our policies will differ from other kingdoms as we are called to reflect the values of the heavenly kingdom here on earth. We work to implement those policies of the kingdom, under the direction of our king. The battles and priorities are His battles, not ours! As He directs the battle, He gives us the resources to accomplish the impossible and the strength and wisdom to do the task immeasurably better than we could comprehend.

The enemy is not my neighbor, the media, the people down the street, or potential terrorists. The enemy is hiding among the citizens and using them as protection. It is a guerrilla war!

We are called to fight—not *against* our neighbors but *for* our neighbors. The battle is to free their bodies, minds, hearts, and souls from bondage and to release them to freedom. Envy, greed, and fear are hard masters, and only God offers freedom from the bondage of the consequences of sin.

The Spirit of the Lord is on me, because he has anointed me to preach good news to the poor. He has sent me to proclaim freedom for the prisoners and recovery of sight for the blind, to set the oppressed free, to proclaim the year of the Lord's favor.

—Luke 4:18–19

The above passage declares freedom from bondage. It is taken from Isaiah 61:1–3 and refers to the year of the Jubilee. In the synagogue, Jesus reads the passage from Isaiah and then sits down. He declares the release of the captives from bondage. Luke 4:18–19 can be seen in several lights. One view is that this is an open declaration of warfare of the Heavenly Kingdom against the principalities and powers of this world. We are called to freedom. We are called as witnesses to exhibit that freedom. The warfare is in relationships. We are called to fight for freedom! It may not be a political freedom. It starts first to free people from spiritual, structural, and philosophical shackles. That battle declaration started two thousand years ago and continues today.

In 1759, William was born in Hull, England, to start his role in the grand cosmic play. He was born to the home of a wealthy merchant and his wife. Nine years later, William's dad died and his mother could no longer take care of him. He was sent to relatives for a few years and then returned to Hull. Eventually he went on to Cambridge, where he spent his time studying cards and immersed himself in the student social life. Somehow he managed to pass his exams. In 1780, at the age of twenty-one and still a student, he managed to be elected as member of House of Commons. He was elected again in 1784. Later that year while on a trip through Europe, he had the opportunity to read *The Rise and Progress of Religion in the Soul* by Philip Doddridge. This time away led to his conversion as a Christian. In 1785, he came to England to attend to matters of Parliament. Later he returned to Europe and then returned a changed man. He was challenged in his lifestyle and his desire to serve God.

During the 1780s, the slave trade was an integral part of the British Economy. Manufactured goods were shipped to Africa, slaves were shipped to the colonies, and commodities were shipped from the colonies back to England. During this time, Quakers and other Christians had started to work towards the abolition of slavery. William was introduced to the cause sometime after his return from Europe. Over time he collected information, made contacts, and then started to work towards the abolition of the slave trade. His strategy was to start with abolishing the slave trade before they could work towards the total abolition of slavery. There were threats and there were many setbacks and delays; however, by the time William Wilberforce died on July 19, 1833, the Slave Trade Act had been passed in 1807 and the Slavery Abolition Act of 1833 had just been passed. William Wilberforce was an agent of change to bring Kingdom values to England and the world. He was one of many called by God to a holy war against injustice. This was a battle, but not one waged with the normal weapons. This was a battle for truth and freedom.

There are concerns with making everything a spiritual battle. We could see everything as a battle between good and evil. We would see ourselves on the good side, of course, and our enemy represents evil. Life is not so black and white, since the evil can be found within. Other times the battle is on the outside. Once it was fought with the traditional weapons of war. Now, as a holy war, it is won on the other side of the gun or the sword. It starts with having victory on the battlefield of our minds and becoming engaged with God and His community to carry us through the battle. The concern over making everything a holy war is that we might have decided on the wrong battle using the wrong plan. It would be like using a map of Venice for a trip to London.

In the first chapter, we covered some history and lessons about holy war. It is a war of God's choice. In the first vignette, Richard realized the enemy was not some faraway Muslim; the battle was more basic and closer to home. He was faced with the consequences of a more basic sin: greed. There is a prescription to deal with envy and greed, but it is not the same plan as the final eternal battle.

In the second vignette, Boray took matters into his own hands. He was motivated by the call to a holy war and the assurance of salvation by dying in battle. He was a witness and a soldier; however, the witness sent the message that Islam is a religion of terrorists that resort to violence to meet their ends. It is a message sent to the west almost every day—that the ends justifies the means until all of the world submits to God through Islam.

The third vignette has Ben struggling on all fronts. He struggles with despair as he works with a fellowship that does not seem engaged in holy war. They seem happy to watch from the stands. As Ben picks up the personal weapons and engages in a call from God, he becomes an effective witness and warrior in the daily battle. The congregation will become engaged, encouraged, and renewed as Ben reflects his love of God in both the personal and public disciplines. He will be victorious in the Holy War as he encourages others and builds the bonds of friendship and fellowship.

Not everything is a holy war. The practical advice in life is to choose your battles. Perhaps more nuanced advice would be to understand your battles. Life is riddled with conflict. We may claim some conflicts to be part of the greater holy war, but in some cases it is just a misunderstanding. It is important to allow some conflicts to be outside of the spiritual battle realm, since God is sovereign and does have ultimate control over the entire universe. We may not understand why bad things happen to good people. In the Old Testament, Job was beset with calamity and painful boils, yet God was in control. There was a spiritual element in the conflict; however, God was still in control and eventually Job was restored. While many of us may not see a spiritual conflict, we could also overcompensate and see Satan behind every attack as we encounter our daily difficulties. It could be the natural result of the curse and living in a broken world. To add some balance to the discussion, I will end with the third verse of *This is My Father's World*, written by Maltbie Babcock in 1901.

> This is my Father's World, O let me ne'er forget.
> That though the wrong seems oft so strong, God is the Ruler yet.
> This is my Father's world: Why should my heart be sad?
> The Lord is King: Let the heavens ring!
> God reigns: let earth be glad!

21. FELLOWSHIP

A FELLOWSHIP IS A GROUP OF PEOPLE WITH A COMMON INTEREST OR GOAL. There is a common friendship bound by a common connection or relationship. In the first book of J.R.R. Tolkien's trilogy, the *Fellowship of the Ring*, a diverse group is brought together under a common mission or cause: to return the ring to be destroyed. The group consisted of hobbits, a dwarf, an elf, and men. The group came from different backgrounds, and had varied strengths and motivations; however, they were knit together with the cause to protect Frodo and to help him on the journey to bring the ring to its final place. We are a company of diverse yet forgiven people bound by the presence of God's Spirit.

> *Let us draw near to God with a sincere heart and with the full assurance that faith brings, having our hearts sprinkled to cleanse us from a guilty conscience and having our bodies washed with pure water. Let us hold unswervingly to the hope we profess, for he who promised is faithful. And let us consider how we may spur one another on toward love and good deeds, not giving up meeting together, as some are in the habit of doing, but encouraging one another—and all the more as you see the Day approaching.*
>
> —Hebrews 10:22–25

The quality of our fellowship is a reflection of our faith and forgiveness. We are in the company of believers, to encourage one another, to build one another up in the faith. The context of the quote from the letter to Hebrews was a call to persevere. There are times when we are weak and the community of believers gives us the strength and encouragement to fight the good fight to the finish. In Paul's letter to the Galatians, we find the origin of the phrase "you reap what you sow."

Do not be deceived: God cannot be mocked. People reap what they sow.
Whoever sows to please their flesh, from their flesh will reap destruction;
whoever sows to please the spirit, from the Spirit will reap eternal life.
Let us not become weary in doing good, for at the proper time we will
reap a harvest if we do not give up.

—Galatians 6:7–9

You reap what you sow, yet earlier in the passage Paul also encourages us to bear one another's burdens. There are times when we are weak and can feel attacked on all sides and we may fail. The community of believers is meant to encourage us in the daily battle.

Brothers and sisters, if someone is caught in sin, you who live by the
Spirit should restore that person gently. But watch yourselves, or you
also may be tempted. Carry each other's burdens, and in this way you
will fulfill the law of Christ.

—Galatians 6:1–2

We are in the company of the faulty and the forgiven! The reality is that in the cosmic play we may lose a battle, or we may be on the verge of losing a battle. It is in the encouragement of others that we may get the strength to persevere and continue the daily struggle. It is in the community that John would gain his strength to "hang on" during the long turmoil of change.

There is a story of Dwight L. Moody going to visit a businessman in Chicago on a cold winter night. He went to encourage him to be an active part of the local church. As they were chatting in front of the warm coal fire, the businessman commented to Dr. Moody that he could be just as good a Christian outside of the church. He did not need to be part of worship. Then Dr. Moody took the tongs and pulled a coal from the fireplace and left it on the hearth. Together they watched as the coal and its embers started to go cold alone as the fire continued to provide light and warmth. "I see," said the businessman.

Proverbs 27:17 says, *"As iron sharpens iron, so one person sharpens another."* As iron sharpens iron, sparks can fly, yet we are to encourage one another until the final days. The fellowship within the church is based on equality and unity, as citizens in the kingdom with a hope to go to the holy city as revealed in Revelation 21. The current values are shaped by the expectation of our arrival to that final destination. The Christian response to Jihad is not a just war or political battle. The holy war starts with the personal preparation of each spiritual soldier. It is a call to personal holiness. It is a call to public distinction. It is a call to encourage one another and to build each other up as workers, witnesses, and warriors under the command of the Eternal King.

The final Hallelujah (Praise to God) will be taken from Psalm 150. The last Psalm also caps this book. We are called as a community and a people to work, and witness, through our worship.

Praise the Lord.
Praise God in his sanctuary;
Praise him in his mighty heavens.
Praise him for his acts of power;
Praise him for him surpassing greatness.
Praise him with the sounding of the trumpet,
Praise him with the harp and lyre,
Praise him with timbrel and dancing,
Praise him with the strings and pipe,
Praise him with the clash of cymbals,
Praise him with resounding cymbals.
Let everything that has breath praise the Lord.
Praise the Lord.

22. BENEDICTION

Heavenly Father, we desire to know you personally and that you may call us Friend.

We thank you for your goodness and mercy, and for your daily provision for us.

We thank you for Jesus Christ, who, as your Son, is our example of how you would have us live, and who also came to be our sacrifice and the gateway to knowing you personally. We acknowledge that we fall short of the mark as a holy people set aside to serve you. We confess that we have been distracted with the props of the play and chasing after things rather than desiring a personal relationship with you.

We thank you for your Holy Spirit, which we invite into our lives, that we may be filled with your presence, your gifts, and the fruit of your presence, that we may be a blessing to others and also to be a gift and blessing to you.

We ask these things in the name of Jesus Christ, your Son and our Savior.

Amen.